THE
NORFOLK
COOKBOOK
SECOND HELPINGS

THE NORFOLK COOK BOOK SECOND HELPINGS

First edition printed in 2023 in the UK
by Bell & Bain Ltd

ISBN: 978-1-915538-15-4

Written by: Katie Fisher, Kate McCann,
Emily Retford & Vicky Frost

Photography by: Katie Hayward

Designed by: Kate McCann, Phil Turner
& Paul Cocker

Sales & PR: Emma Toogood & Lizzy Capps

Published by Meze Publishing Limited
Unit 1b, 2 Kelham Square
Kelham Riverside
Sheffield S3 8SD
Web: www.mezepublishing.co.uk
Telephone: 0114 275 7709
Email: info@mezepublishing.co.uk

WELCOME BACK FOR SECONDS!

In 2017, we launched our first Norfolk Cook Book, celebrating the county's amazing independent food and drink scene. Since then, things have developed so much that we've put together a follow up to showcase more of the brilliant cafés, restaurants, producers, pubs, coffee shops, bars and bakeries that grace this wonderful county.

With more than 30 recipes to try at home, this book is packed with culinary goodness as well as serving as a helpful guide to the region's best foodie hangouts. We think that food and drink tastes better when you know how much love and dedication goes into it, so we've caught up with all the lovely people who generously shared their signature dishes, desserts and cocktails to tell their stories too.

For those in the know, it's hard to beat Norfolk's incredible array of small businesses, whether you're after a pie and a pint or a fine dining experience. Many are run by families and artisans who are not just about turning a profit but creating the best food and drink they possibly can. Often they'll use ingredients grown, reared, distilled and produced within the county and its surrounding countryside, creating a network of supportive independents who collaborate and innovate.

One thing they all have in common is the pride in what Norfolk is, has been, and can become. And what better way to be part of that exciting future than indulging in everything the region has to offer?

So whether you're a local with a good grasp of Norfolk's food and drink scene already, new to the area or just passing through, it's time to sit down, take a moment and get stuck in.

TEAM MEZE X

CONTENTS

FROM BEEF BURGERS TO BEEF RENDANG

Combining Asian-inspired dishes and street food classics with quality Norfolk ingredients, The Cabin is a unique street food business that has something for everyone.

The Cabin is a Norfolk-based street food business that serves delicious, Asian-inspired food from their taco caravan. Justin, The Cabin's owner, hand cooks every meal and ensures that all of the produce is only Norfolk's very best. He takes a unique and creative approach to tacos and rice boxes that results in a memorable dish for each customer.

The team is passionate about quality, local ingredients and sourcing from sustainable farms. Their key supplier of rare breed lamb and pork is Edfords Care Farm (@edfordscarefarm), a not-for-profit organisation that also offers therapeutic and educational services. Using only the best produce, The Cabin creates vibrant and flavourful dishes such as Lamb Rendang, Sri Lankan Chicken, and Vegan Sweet Potato, Chickpea and Spinach Laksa. Asian-inspired dishes aside, The Cabin also serves American-style street food such as burgers and fries.

This style of street food is where The Cabin's roots lie, having begun as a converted 80s Avondale caravan that at first served only tacos, wings and fries. Justin founded the business himself after a vast career of culinary experience, including a partnership in London's Spit&Roast, a 12-year long ownership of his self-started restaurant in Exmouth Market, and culinary training in France. He has traded at several festivals including Glastonbury, Houghton, Red Rooster, Wildpaths and Gunton Arms Festival. Despite the challenges of lockdown, The Cabin was also chosen to be part of the very successful weekly street food market based near Holt, @streetfoodmarketatthepigs.

Now, Justin's passion for cooking great quality street food drives the business. After three years of trading, The Cabin is very well established as a top-quality trader in North Norfolk and has had a productive year, with glowing feedback from their social media platforms.

BEEF RENDANG

Preparation time: 30 minutes | Cooking time: 2 hours | Serves 6

We are blessed with the best beef in Norfolk courtesy of our outstanding butcher, Arthur Howell of Wells. This beef dish was originally from Malaysia/Indonesia and was used as a way to preserve meat without refrigeration. The meat would be cooked down with the delicious and fragrant rendang spices and coconut milk, then sealed with its own fat in clay pots and buried to keep cool.

For the rendang paste

2 tbsp roughly chopped shallot

2 tbsp roughly chopped garlic

2 tbsp roughly chopped ginger

2 tbsp roughly chopped galangal

2 tbsp roughly chopped lemongrass

2 tbsp roughly chopped kaffir lime leaf

1 tbsp roughly chopped cinnamon stick

2 tbsp tamarind paste

2 tbsp sugar

2 tbsp dried red chilli

1 tbsp ground cardamom

For the beef

2 tbsp coconut oil

2 tins of coconut milk

1 kg finest Norfolk braising beef, diced

Blitz all of the paste ingredients together for 20 seconds. A Nutribullet or similar is best for this. In a frying pan, heat the coconut oil. Add the paste to the pan and cook gently until the oil splits out.

At this point, add the coconut milk and cook out for 10 minutes.

Add the beef and cook on a slow simmer for 2 hours or until three quarters of the liquid has been absorbed.

Season with salt and pepper to taste. We add nam pla (fish sauce) as a seasoning as well.

RAISE A GLASS FOR NORFOLK WINE!

Tucked away in rural South Norfolk, the family-run Chet Valley Vineyard produces award-winning wines of exceptional quality and offers unforgettable experiences. Actively involved in conservation projects, the Chet Valley Vineyard stands alone as an accredited sustainable wine producer for the area.

Winemaker John Hemmant first started growing and fermenting grapes in the late eighties, making him one of the most experienced, and decorated winemakers in the country. Since then, Chet Valley wines have won numerous medals including a Decanter World Wine Award and International World Challenge.

Chet Valley is a friendly and welcoming family-run business yet maintains a classy and sophisticated atmosphere. Their success is dependent on the responsibilities of the family and their close friends, from picking the grapes by hand to running their social media accounts. Every year the grape harvest is gathered in by volunteers from the close-knit community: some experienced helpers who return each year for fun and friendship, and many who come just for one day to enjoy the festive atmosphere and fresh October air.

The Chet Valley Vineyard has recently been named among few accredited Sustainable Wine Producers of Great Britain, demonstrating responsible land management, support for biodiversity and reduced carbon emissions. The vineyard has been the site of several ecological studies by scientists at the UEA, has worked with the Bergh Apton Conservation Trust to plant extensive hedging, and representatives from Bergh Apton and Alpington primary school came to the site to plant trees.

There are many opportunities for visitors to come and enjoy this unspoilt countryside, including vine leasing, wine club membership and volunteering to pick grapes in the autumn. Visitors can experience the Chet Valley Vineyard's ten wines through formal tastings which are recommended to help customers orientate themselves, for the personal aromas and taste.

The Chet Valley Vineyard prides itself on its magnificent wines. The eponymous wines, House of Hemmant Blanc de Noirs, Blanc de Blancs and Skylark, are made in the same way as Champagne – that is, secondary fermentation in a sealed bottle. The other wines from the vineyard are named after songbirds that frequent the site, including finches, linnets, robins, and redwings.

The Chet Vineyard is pleased to announce that the Wine Meadow is now open on site, a beautiful seating area including a balcony to look out over the vineyards, a picturesque pond and a converted horsebox bar, making it the perfect site for parties, celebrations and pop-up food events.

SUMMER CELEBRATION GÂTEAU

Preparation time: 30 minutes | Cooking time: 15-20 minutes | Serves 10

This cake is the ultimate treat to serve with a Chet Valley Vineyard sparkling wine. It's the perfect gift to make for someone you love, and this delicious dessert is low in fat! Enjoy!

4 eggs

150g caster sugar

1 lemon, zested

100g plain flour

For the filling

300g low-fat soft cheese

90g caster sugar

120g low-fat fromage frais (or for a full-fat version, 300ml double cream will do just fine!)

1 lemon, juiced

500g strawberries

50g chopped almonds, toasted

Preheat the oven to 190°c. Grease and line a 40x30cm Swiss roll tin.

In a bowl, whisk the eggs, sugar, and lemon zest together with a handheld electric whisk until the mixture doubles in size and a trail remains on the surface for 15 seconds. This takes at least 10 minutes.

Fold in the flour with a metal spoon, being careful not to knock out the air. Pour into the tin and bake for 15-20 minutes, or until the cake springs back when lightly pressed. Remove from the oven, turn out the cake onto a wire rack, and leave to cool.

To make the filling, in a separate bowl, mix the soft cheese with the sugar and fromage frais. Add the lemon juice and mix well. Divide the filling into two bowls. Chop half the strawberries and mix these into one bowl. Leave the other plain.

Cut the sponge widthways into 3 equal pieces and sandwich these together with the strawberry filling. Spread two thirds of the plain filling over the sides of the cake and press on the toasted almonds.

Spread the rest of the plain filling over the top of the gâteau and decorate with strawberry halves.

To serve

Dust with icing sugar.

A CRÊPE FOR EVERY OCCASION

Chris has developed his love for crêpes into his very own crêperie, selling both sweet and savoury pancakes from his Pottergate café.

Christophe's Crêpes is an independent crêperie that began in 2011 when Chris decided to take his passion for crêpes to a business level. Offering both savoury and sweet crêpes at their café in Pottergate, Christophe's Crêpes is perfect for either a sit-down or a takeaway pancake. It has quickly become a local favourite, being named the top spot in Norwich for pancakes on Pancake Day by the Norwich Evening News. It's not just for Pancake Day though; you can try their delicious crêpes throughout the year.

Pancakes have always been one of Chris' favourite foods. His passion for them began as a child when his nan would cook them, and developed during trips to Europe with his wife. These European trips inspired Chris to pursue crêpes as a career, cooking them at events and weddings, and eventually earning himself a permanent spot on Davey Place with his own crêpe van.

For ten years, Chris ran his crêpe van with the dream of one day owning a shop of his own, and this dream materialised in 2020. With the arrival of Covid and lockdowns just after Chris opened his shop, there were uncertain times ahead. However, his determination and love for his business inspired him to continue, resulting in queues of people in facemasks lining up for one of Christophe's crêpes, for which Chris says he will be "forever grateful".

The shop in Pottergate has now been running for just over three years, and feels like home for Chris, who feels proud to be part of Norwich's thriving community of independent businesses. Pop round to try the classic Lemon and Sugar crêpe, or if you don't have much of a sweet tooth, their best-selling Luigi crêpe, filled with cheddar, mozzarella, fresh pesto, baby leaf spinach, chopped baby plum tomatoes, and bacon.

CHRISTOPHE'S CRÊPE SAUCES AND FILLINGS

Preparation time: 5 minutes each | Cooking time: 15 minutes each

These two recipes are perfect accompaniments to crêpes of any kind. The first recipe, our simple and fresh cranberry sauce, is delicious in our Cran-Brie crêpe with French brie, smoked bacon, and baby leaf spinach. We make it every autumn! The second recipe, our sweet stovetop apple filling, is perfect in our famous Cinapple crêpe. Why not make your own crêpes to go with these tasty sauces?

For the Cranberry Crêpe Sauce

100ml pure orange juice

100g light muscovado sugar

250g fresh cranberries

Juice of ½ a lemon

For the Stovetop Apple Filling

1 tbsp salted butter

80ml water

4 apples, skins removed and sliced

2 tbsp cornflour

2 tbsp demerara sugar

¾ tbsp cinnamon

Cranberry Crêpe Sauce

Firstly, put the orange juice in a saucepan and bring to the boil. Then, stir in the sugar.

Add the cranberries and gently stir them in. Leave to simmer for approximately 5 minutes - you want the cranberries to still have shape but to be nice and soft. Then, add the lemon juice while the mixture is cooling and mix.

Let the sauce cool - you will see it start to thicken. Use immediately on freshly cooked crêpes, or store in the fridge (it lasts for up to a week). It's that easy and delicious!

Stovetop Apple Filling

Place the butter in a sauté pan or a large frying pan with just a teaspoon of water on medium heat. Once melted, add the sliced apples. We cut them more into chunks, as this makes them easier to eat in a crêpe but slices also work well. Stir the apples to coat them in butter and leave to cook for 5 minutes.

In a bowl, mix the cornflour and the 80ml of water until they become a paste.

In a separate bowl, mix the sugar and cinnamon.

Add both mixtures to the pan with the butter and apples. Mix everything and simmer for 4-5 minutes until the apples are tender and the sauce is a nice consistency. Then, take it off the heat. It will get thicker as it cools. Serve immediately with a freshly cooked crêpe and enjoy!

IT'S AN ESTATE OF MIND

A destination for family dining and much more, the Elveden Estate is all about the very best local food, from potatoes grown on its own farmland to venison managed and butchered on site.

The Elveden Estate is a mecca for local and regional food in Norfolk. The Elveden Courtyard – with its restaurant, shops and dog-friendly café – and The Elveden Inn are both situated on the estate, a 22,000-acre expanse of largely farmland that has been home to the Guinness family since the end of the 19th century. They grow their own potatoes, carrots and onions as well as producing venison and game, managed by the game and conservation departments who look after the estate. This homegrown produce features on the mouth-watering menus at both venues, giving the Courtyard and the Inn a well-deserved reputation as a hub of delicious local food.

Mark Elvin, Elveden Estate's head chef, creates seasonal dishes that change throughout the year, always using local ingredients wherever possible. Expect classic dishes with a modern twist such as their Venison Scotch Egg alongside firm favourites including traditional roast beef, fish and chips, hearty casseroles and much more. The restaurants at both venues use produce sourced from the estate and the surrounding areas, helped by the on-site butchery at Elveden Courtyard which ensures they have the freshest cuts available and even makes the burgers in house.

The estate as it is today was developed with the intention of opening a farm shop and restaurant to sell and prepare Elveden's and Norfolk's wonderful food. Visitors can enjoy the success of this vision throughout the year and even stay in beautifully decorated rooms at The Elveden Inn for a countryside getaway. The restaurants have a family-friendly atmosphere, with dog-friendly options at both sites, and The Courtyard includes a play area, making sure the estate can be enjoyed by all. Handily located just off the A11 and a few minutes drive from the nearby Elveden Center Parcs, the estate has established itself as a foodie destination for Norfolk to be proud of.

VENISON WITH CARROT KETCHUP AND CONFIT POTATO

Preparation time: 30 minutes | Cooking time: 30 minutes | Serves 2

This starter is based on produce from the Elveden Estate; beautiful venison, carrots and potatoes
are paired with earthy beetroot, tangy blackberries and a nutty crunch from the hazelnuts.
– Mark Elvin, Elveden Courtyard.

260g venison loin, trimmed
Rapeseed oil

For the beetroot
3 baby beetroot
300ml orange juice
1 sprig of thyme
2 star anise

For the confit potato
1 medium potato
500g beef dripping
3 cloves of garlic, crushed
1 sprig of rosemary, chopped

For the carrot ketchup
2 medium carrots, grated
½ white onion, diced small
150g apple juice
100g water
30g maple syrup
22g apple cider vinegar
2g each of smoked paprika, grated
nutmeg, ground cumin and ground
cinnamon

To serve
6 fresh blackberries
8 blanched hazelnuts, crushed

For the beetroot
Place the beetroot in the orange juice with thyme and star anise, then simmer until tender. Peel the skins off and put the beetroot to one side.

For the confit potato
Peel the potato and then use a metal pastry cutter to cut it into small discs. Place the discs in a small pan on a medium heat and colour on both sides. Add the beef dripping, garlic and rosemary. Cook on a low heat until the potato is soft and cooked through. Leave to cool in the pan.

For the carrot ketchup
Add all the ingredients to a pan and simmer for 25 minutes. When the carrots are soft, place the mixture in a blender and blitz until smooth. Add salt to taste. Chef's Tip: For a thicker ketchup, reduce the mixture for longer in the pan. This can be served warm or cold.

For the venison
Get a frying pan hot and drizzle it with rapeseed oil. Place the venison in the pan and sear on all sides. Season well with salt and pepper. Add the cooked beetroot to the same pan, then place the pan in a preheated oven at 190°c for 8 minutes. Remove and set aside to rest for 10 minutes.

To serve
Slice the rested venison loin in half. Place the confit potato and beetroot on the plate, then garnish with the carrot ketchup, blackberries and crushed hazelnuts.

ROASTED HAKE WITH GNOCCHI AND ROMESCO SAUCE

Preparation time: 30 minutes | Cooking time: 30 minutes | Serves 4

I've chosen to share this dish for its combination of subtle flavours. It also incorporates a member of the cod family, hake, which I feel is quite underrated. This recipe is best with skin-on hake fillets, descaled by your fishmonger. – Jon Curtis, The Elveden Inn

4 x 140g hake fillets

200g cavolo nero

Butter

For the Romesco sauce

2 red peppers

Vegetable oil

Salt and pepper

400g vine tomatoes

20ml white wine vinegar

4 cloves of garlic, peeled and finely chopped

5g white sugar

20g ground almonds

1 tsp smoked sweet paprika

For the gnocchi

375g warm mashed potato (we make ours from baked Elveden potatoes put through a ricer)

75g 00 flour

2 egg yolks

Salt, to taste

For the Romesco sauce

Preheat your oven to 200°c. Rub the peppers with vegetable oil, season with salt and pepper to taste, then roast in the oven for 20 minutes. At the same time, roast the tomatoes on a separate tray in the oven.

Transfer the roasted peppers to a bowl, cover with cling film and leave for 20 minutes to steam and loosen the skins. Set a sieve over a clean bowl and peel the peppers, discarding the seeds and skin, over the sieve to catch any juices.

In a small pan, gently heat the vinegar with the garlic and white sugar until the liquid has reduced by half. Pour this into a blender along with the prepared peppers (including the reserved juices) and roasted tomatoes. Add the ground almonds and paprika, then blend until super smooth. Season the Romesco sauce with salt and pepper to taste and set aside until needed.

For the gnocchi

Gently mix all the ingredients together to form a dough, then roll out on a floured surface to the thickness of a finger. Do this in small batches. Cut the dough into 20mm pieces and transfer to a floured tray. Drop the gnocchi into a pan of salted boiling water to cook for 2 minutes, then carefully lift out with a slotted spoon and cool in iced water. Drain the gnocchi once cool.

To assemble the dish

Preheat the oven to 200°c and put a frying pan on the heat with a light covering of oil in. Season the hake fillets with salt and pepper, then place skin side down in the hot pan to cook for 5 minutes. Turn the fillets over, then place the pan in the oven for 4 minutes. Remove and rest the fish.

Meanwhile, gently warm up the Romesco sauce. Trim the cavolo nero and cook for 2 minutes in a pan with a knob of butter. Season to taste with salt and pepper, then drain off the excess liquid. Pan fry the gnocchi in a non-stick frying pan with butter and oil, turning them frequently until golden all over, then transfer to kitchen paper.

Swipe the Romesco sauce across warm plates, then place the hake fillet on top surrounded by cavolo nero and gnocchi. Serve immediately.

CHOCOLATE AND GUINNESS CAKE

Preparation time: 30 minutes, plus freezing and cooling | Cooking time: 40 minutes | Serves 12-14

Elveden Estate is the home of the Guinness family, and that history is the inspiration behind this dessert: a beautifully rich and malty sponge served with tangy shards of frozen cream cheese, a caramelised white chocolate crumb, and fresh Norfolk raspberries. – Mark Elvin, Elveden Courtyard

For the cake
300ml Guinness
200g butter
150g dark chocolate
500g soft light brown sugar
4 medium eggs
350g self-raising flour

For the frozen cream cheese
120g full-fat cream cheese
25g caster sugar

For the caramelised white chocolate crumb
200g white chocolate

To serve
1 punnet of Norfolk raspberries

For the cake
Heat the Guinness, butter and chocolate in a bain-marie, stirring until smooth and melted together. Let this mixture cool slightly, then add the sugar and eggs. Mix well. Fold in the flour until just combined. Pour the cake mixture into a lined tin or tray, then bake for 40 minutes at 160°c. Carefully turn out to cool on a wire rack, then slice into 14 portions before serving.

For the frozen cream cheese
Beat the cream cheese and sugar together, then spread the mixture on a tray lined with greaseproof paper. Place in the freezer and freeze until solid. Break the frozen cream cheese into pieces and store in a covered container in the freezer until needed.

For the caramelised white chocolate crumb
Place the chocolate on a non-stick tray in a preheated oven at 190°c. Bake until the chocolate starts to caramelise and darken in colour, then remove and leave to cool completely. Make sure the chocolate is completely cold before breaking up and blitzing in a food processor. This will form a crumb which can be stored at room temperature until needed.

To serve
Plate portions of the cake with frozen cream cheese pieces, caramelised white chocolate crumb, and fresh raspberries arranged decoratively around them.

FARM PRODUCE AT ITS FINEST

Michelin listed, Norwich-based restaurant FARMYARD prides itself on fine produce, not fine dining, and cares as much about their 'free-range chefs' as the high quality and sustainable produce.

Husband and wife duo Andrew Jones and Hannah Springham moved home to Norfolk and opened their Norwich-based restaurant FARMYARD in 2017 to rapid critical acclaim. Six years on, the restaurant has been listed in the Michelin Guide, visited and praised by Jay Rayner, and awarded three AA rosettes. The initial concept of FARMYARD was led by chef patron Andrew's dream of celebrating the best of Norfolk's farm produce without the fuss or ego often found in gastronomy.

Their slogan – refined food with attitude – means fine produce, not fine dining. FARMYARD work directly with farmers and producers who supply them with the best their region has to offer each season. Meats come from FARMYARD's favourite farmer Rob at Swannington Farm to Fork, Fen Farm Dairy provides some incredible cheeses, and Hannah from Eveshill grows bespoke herbs and salads for the restaurant each season, to give just a few examples.

The chefs cook over sustainably sourced charcoal on their Bertha oven to give this handpicked produce a unique flavour. It's all about the ingredients they get handed each week, which dictate the menu, and creating a restaurant that feels welcoming and fun (without a white tablecloth in sight). The food is unfussy bistro-style fare, using gastronomic flavours and techniques but served in the most unpretentious way. Customers especially love The FARMYARD Chocolate Bar, the sharing Cote De Boeuf Steak and the daily changing set menu.

In addition to the restaurant, during lockdown the family launched a restaurant-level range of frozen food 'for foodies' which is handcrafted in Norfolk by their restaurant chefs before being delivered nationally and sold in around 30 local stockists. FARMYARD Frozen is the thinking person's frozen food product with the quality to back up the hype, thanks to the handcrafted, indulgent and affordable dishes that are designed to recreate a bistro feel at home.

Another aspect of the restaurant that sets FARMYARD apart is their 'Happy Hospitality' policy, which was also implemented following the pandemic and means their chefs work no more than a four-day week. This ensures they can avoid burnout, improve wellbeing, and ultimately help the whole team provide guests with memorable experiences at this celebration of Norfolk's finest farm produce.

DEEP FRIED BARON BIGOD AND BURNT APPLE PURÉE

Preparation time: 20-30 minutes | Cooking time: 30-40 minutes | Serves 4 as a starter

We love Baron Bigod at FARMYARD; it's always on the cheeseboard. This is a little reboot of the classic starter served with a tangy, rich burnt apple purée. Our crispy Baron Bigod starter within the FARMYARD frozen range is one of our best sellers; now you can have a go at recreating some of our mouth-watering magic at home.

For the deep fried Baron Bigod

1 Baby Baron (you can use Truffled Baron if you're feeling extra luxurious)

120g plain flour

Pinch of salt

Pinch of black pepper

2 eggs

Splash of milk

120g panko breadcrumbs

Neutral oil for deep-frying (vegetable oil is best)

For the burnt apple purée

6 apples (Cox, Bramley, Granny Smith or any variety with a good tart edge is best)

2 tbsp demerara sugar

Pinch of salt

Pinch of cayenne pepper or chilli flakes

2 tbsp sherry vinegar

For the deep fried Baron Bigod

Cut the Baby Baron into 8 equal wedges and chill in the fridge. In a shallow dish, mix the flour, salt, and black pepper together. In another shallow dish, beat the eggs with a splash of milk. Place the panko breadcrumbs in a third shallow dish.

Dip each wedge of chilled cheese into the seasoned flour mixture, then shake off any excess. Next, dip the floured wedges into the beaten egg, making sure to coat them thoroughly. Finally, coat the wedges with the panko breadcrumbs, then return to the fridge until needed.

Heat the oil to 180°c in a deep fat fryer or large pan. Fry the breadcrumbed Baron wedges in batches for 2-3 minutes, or until golden brown and crispy on all sides. Remove them from the oil with a slotted spoon and place on a plate lined with paper towels to drain any excess oil.

For the burnt apple purée

This is a great condiment for all sorts of dishes. It works really well with cold meats or just on a cheese sandwich. Blackening the apples adds a great depth and complexity, while a tingle of heat from the chilli gives it a bit of zing. If you have some smoked chipotle chillies to blend with the apple, this will add another layer of flavour too.

Preheat your oven to 220°c/200°c fan/gas mark 7. Core and halve the apples, place on a baking tray and sprinkle them with the sugar, salt, and cayenne or chilli flakes. Roast the apples in the preheated oven until they are well caramelised and catching around the edges.

Remove the apples from the oven and let them cool slightly. Deglaze the roasting pan with the sherry vinegar to remove all the caramel while it's still hot.

Blend the apples with the vinegar from the pan in a blender or food processor until you have a smooth purée. Taste and adjust the seasoning with additional vinegar, sugar or salt as needed.

To serve

Plate two wedges of crispy fried Baron Bigod per person as soon as it has drained, along with a generous spoonful of the burnt apple purée on each plate.

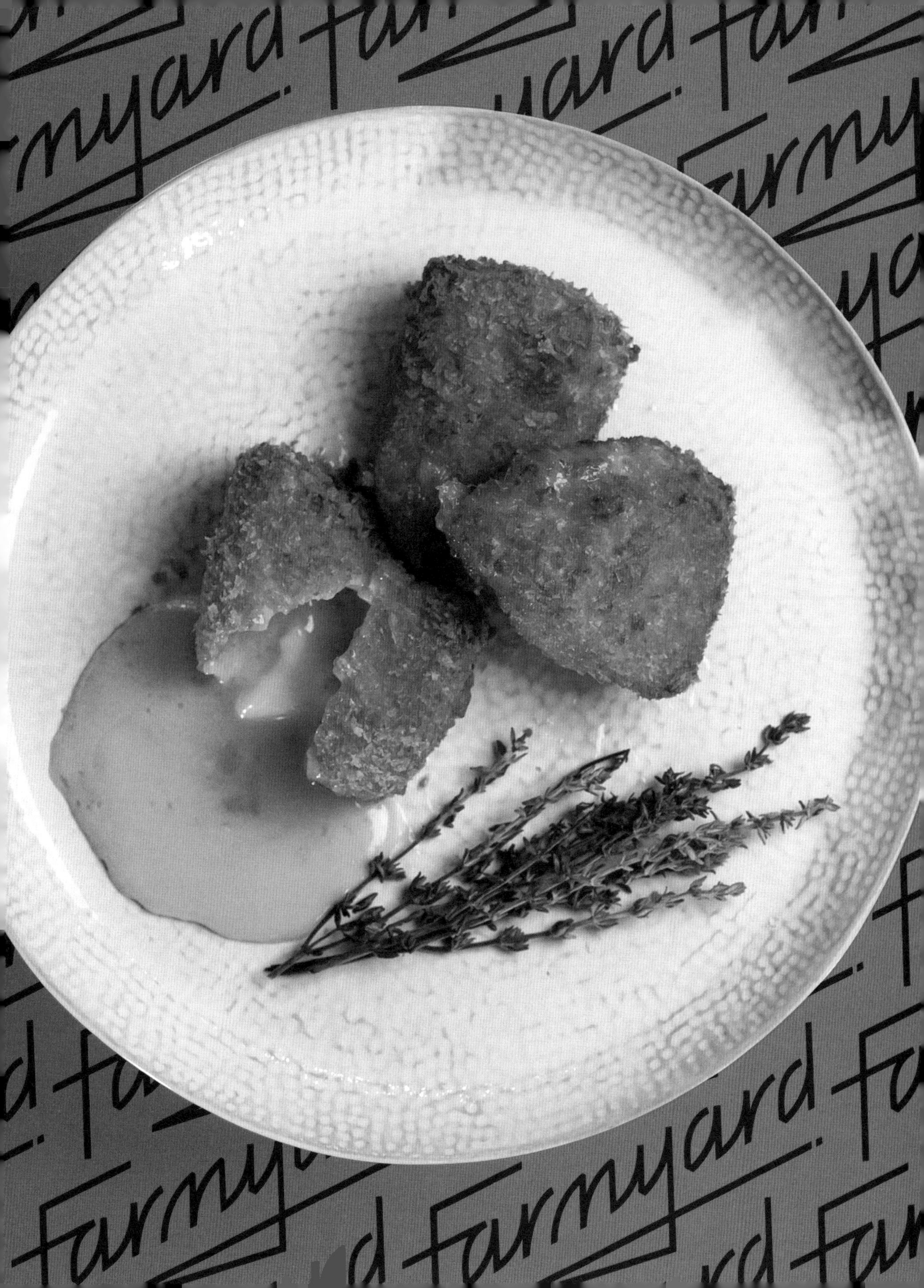
Farmyard

THE SWEETER SIDE OF LIFE

Laid back yet lively Figbar is a must-visit for dessert fans everywhere. Whether you're popping in for a sweet treat or sampling the full plated dessert selection with an assiette, your favourite flavours are waiting.

Award-winning Figbar is the restaurant of experienced pastry chef Jaime Garbutt. It features a masterfully designed plated dessert menu which draws on Chef Garbutt's extensive pastry background working for Gordon Ramsay, Marcus Wareing, Galton Blackiston, and the Ottolenghi Group before helping to establish the renowned Playboy Club London and Jinjuu Group with American celebrity chef Judy Joo.

Established in 2016, Figbar began its life as and continues to be a small family-run business. The concept centres on sophisticated plated desserts and high-end cakes and pastries. Every element of each item is made in-house by Chef Garbutt and his highly trained team. Visitors can expect to find a dessert menu that rivals Michelin–starred restaurants (and Chef Garbutt has worked in a few!) as well as a counter full of sweet treats, all developed and made in-house. Figbar favourites include chocolate and fudge 'hobnobs', funfetti cake, banana buck-eye cake, rosemary chocolate chip cookie bars, and twice-baked chocolate torte. Weekend specials include yuzu meringue choux buns, cinnamon buns with cream cheese icing, and egg custard tart. There is even a mini-fridge stocked with take-away dessert pots.

With so much to choose from, it's no wonder that Figbar is regularly booked up on Friday and Saturday evenings, while also being a popular coffee and cake spot in the daytime for sitting in or taking away. The team offers wedding and occasion catering, wholesale options, and they even create custom menus with drinks pairings for private bookings for those who want the 20-seater venue all to themselves. With a well-deserved reputation for excellence, guests can see its mission statement in action: amplify your sweet tooth. With an ever-changing menu using ingredients that draw inspiration from the seasons, colour palettes, and even childhood treats, you never know what new creations may appear.

There's a broad range of dessert wines to sip on too, as well as beer, Scotch, cognac, Port, sherry, and spirits, pairing with the plated dessert menu wonderfully. Gluten-free and vegan guests are always catered for, and visitors can watch their desserts being plated up in the open kitchen. Chef Garbutt and his family are integral to the success of this clever niche in Norfolk's food scene, and they continue to innovate; 2023 was the first year they were able to use entirely British-grown sugar in the kitchen. Simply put, at Figbar you will find a haven for anyone with a sweet tooth.

Figbar

biscuit tea
brown sugar | lady grey | malt | lemon | milk
8.5/16.5

disznoko late harvest tokaji
sweet | tropical fruit | spice

snickers
chocolate | peanut | caramel | salt
7.5/13

growers touch cabernet sauvignon
red fruit | berries | warm bodied

strawberries
pea | gin | lemon | basil | elderflower | meringue
7.5/16.5

casa defra prosecco
ripe white fruit | light sweetness

passion fruit
chocolate | passion fruit | coconut | tonka
8.5/14

tierra del rey sauvignon blanc
grapefruit | lime | ripe melon

assiette selection 30

pie of the week 7
served with home-made vanilla soft serve

sundae of the week 7
home-made vanilla soft serve with toppings

A DELI WITH A DIFFERENCE

With fresh ideas and delicious food always on the menu, SALT is more than a lunch stop: not least thanks to their irresistible winter raclette season!

Chef Jaime Garbutt and his wife Stephanie have created two thriving businesses in central Norwich that complement each other perfectly: dessert bar Figbar began their sweet life in the fine city and savoury SALT seasoned their corner of the historic Norwich Lanes. SALT was established in 2019 as a companion to its sister restaurant Figbar and offers a daytime deli that boasts sandwiches, salads, soups, and grilled cheeses for the lunch crowd. Plus, who could resist breakfast options like banana bread and freshly baked cinnamon buns?

By working seasonally for the best quality produce and ingredients, SALT is able to make almost everything in-house as well as supporting local bakeries, coffee roasters, and tea merchants for the Norfolk touch. The flavours, however, are anything but local: Chef Garbutt's extensive travels during his career as a professional chef and Stephanie's American background keeps the daily offering full of excitement. Having lived and worked in Asia, from Korea to Hong Kong, as well as his London restaurant background (including Gordon Ramsay, Marcus Wareing, Yotam Ottolenghi, and the Jinjuu Group), he has plenty of experience to draw on. Mediterranean and Middle Eastern food is a big part of the SALT ethos too; fresh vegetables and pulses abound in creative salads that feature layers of flavour and texture.

Every year between September and December, SALT runs a hugely popular raclette menu on Friday and Saturday evenings with irresistible variations on the traditional après ski indulgence. The classic melted raclette cheese over roasted potatoes is always a winner, but extras such as braised oxtail chilli, wild truffle and garlic mushrooms, or ratatouille make their raclettes truly one of a kind.

As both an essential seasoning and one of Norwich's most exciting eateries, where would we be without SALT?

BASBOUSA, WHIPPED YOGHURT, TURKISH RHUBARB, PISTACHIOS

Preparation time: 30 minutes | Cooking time: 1 hour | Serves 8

Basbousa is a floral Egyptian syrup cake that pairs beautifully with tangy yoghurt and the slight sourness of English rhubarb. Perfect for an indulgent afternoon treat with tea or as a dinner party pud with coffee.

For the basbousa

190g ground semolina

100g plain flour

70g golden caster sugar

70g desiccated coconut

15g baking powder

10g ground pistachios

170g each of marmalade and oil

4 eggs

4 oranges, zested and juiced (250ml)

For the syrup

200g sugar

50g orange blossom water

1 lemon, zested and juiced

For the whipped yoghurt

300g double cream

150g Greek yoghurt

50g icing sugar

1 tsp vanilla extract

Zest of 1 lemon

For the rhubarb

100g sugar

4 sticks of rhubarb

1 tbsp each of grenadine and rose water

1 lemon, zested and juiced

100g chopped green pistachios

For the basbousa and the syrup

In a large bowl, combine the semolina, flour, sugar, coconut, baking powder, and ground pistachios. In a jug, whisk the marmalade, oil, eggs, orange juice and orange zest together. Add the wet ingredients to the dry and slowly whisk together until just combined. Do not overmix.

Pour the batter into an 8-inch lined cake tray and place in a preheated oven at 165°c for about 55 minutes until the cake is golden on top and a knife inserted into the middle comes out hot and dry. While the cake is in the oven, make the syrup. Place the sugar and 100ml of water into a small saucepan over a medium heat. Bring to the boil and then add the orange blossom water, lemon juice and lemon zest.

Immediately pour the syrup over the hot cake once it comes out the oven. Set aside to cool.

For the whipped yoghurt

Place the ingredients in a mixing bowl and whisk until firm. Chill until required.

For the rhubarb

Preheat the oven to 150°c. Pour the sugar into an ovenproof dish. Cut the rhubarb into 3cm long pieces and lay them close together over the sugar. Pour over the grenadine, rose water, lemon zest and lemon juice, along with 50ml of water, then bake until rhubarb is soft but holding its shape, around 20 minutes. Check regularly as it will go from cooked to mush really quickly. Allow to cool fully.

To serve

Once cooled, cut the basbaousa into 8-12 wedges and place on plates with a dollop of the yoghurt and a few slices of rhubarb. Decorate with the chopped green pistachios, then serve and enjoy!

A RESTAURANT WITH HERITAGE

The Ingham Swan is an award-winning food-driven restaurant in the quiet countryside, offering seven contemporary 4-star bedrooms, just minutes from the Norfolk coastline and the Broads. Led by Chef Patron Daniel Smith, the restaurant offers the perfect food-led overnight experience.

The Ingham Swan sits in the rural village of Ingham, just minutes from the stunning Northeast Norfolk coastline, near Sea Palling. Originally built as a Coaching Inn in the 14th Century, the pretty thatched building has been a popular relaxed fine dining restaurant since 2010 under the direction and ownership of Chef Patron Daniel Smith. It was carefully refurbished in 2017 following a devastating fire. Chef Daniel also oversees South Norfolk's The Wildebeest, another award-winning, Michelin Recommended restaurant, which he purchased in 2015.

Located next to Holy Trinity Church in a quiet, peaceful setting, there's space to breathe and views around every corner. There are seven contemporary rooms that provide overnight accommodation for the perfect Stay & Dine experience. The building itself is warm and welcoming with an intimate interior. It has, after all, been welcoming people for centuries. The interior style has been overseen by London-based designer Kathryn Mazure-Hudson and features brass, beautiful herringbone wood, marble and velvet - all working beautifully with the original beams and Norfolk flint.

With a reputation as one of Norfolk's most trusted and creative chefs, Daniel has a long-spanning career, holding multiple accolades including Norfolk Chef of the Year 2014, Chef of the Year - Craft Guild of Chefs Awards 2017 and taking part in BBC2's Great British Menu 2016. He and his team are passionate about food that is focused on Norfolk's rich bounty of local produce that is available on the doorstep, bringing together dishes that embrace every season with daily changing and locally inspired menus, working with trusted suppliers who offer quality ingredients. The Michelin Recommended fine dining business, with 3AA Rosettes, operates in a relaxed setting where they live and love the finest, freshest food with a cast-iron commitment to seasonality in their simple yet delectable food.

Dishes include many Ingham Swan diners' favourites, as well as brand new dishes including ideas and flavours from Daniel's time on BBC2's Great British Menu. Wine pairing service is also available to enjoy alongside delicious Taster Menus. "Our kitchen explores and showcases the very best ingredients. We work hard to ensure that every dish leaving the kitchen is prepared, cooked and presented to perfection."

DANIEL'S RASPBERRY SET CREAM

Preparation time: 45 minutes, plus 6 hours chilling time | Serves 8

A stunningly simple, seasonal dessert, ideal for a summer party, created by Chef Patron Daniel Smith. "Everything I serve from the kitchen takes its cue from the current season and that's why this summer dessert is a particular favourite of mine using summer's freshest berries." You could also adapt this recipe to use strawberries or blackberries when they are at their best.

500ml raspberry purée (homemade or store-bought)

500ml double cream

120g caster sugar

3 leaves of bronze gelatine, soaked in cold water

Place the raspberry purée, double cream, and sugar into a pan. Bring to the boil then aside to cool. Squeeze out the gelatine and add to the pan. Stir to dissolve.

Pour the liquid into ramekins or moulds and chill in the fridge until set.

To serve

Serve with fresh berries and garnish with a sprig of mint if you like. And why not add a scoop of ice cream of your choice? For that extra touch, honeycomb makes a lovely addition. If you haven't made honeycomb before, a simple cheat is to add some Crunchie Bar or good quality shop-bought honeycomb.

Chef's Tip

While your berries might look perfect, their flavour is not always guaranteed. You might want to consider marinating your berries beforehand using a combination of stock syrup with an alcohol of your choice (something like Cointreau, perhaps). This process will sweeten up any sharper berries you might have for your purée.

THE BEST KFC IN NORFOLK!

For freshly prepared, deliciously authentic Korean food in Norwich, look no further than The Kimchi to enjoy a cosy and casual dining experience.

After years of extensive culinary studies at William Angliss Cookery College in Melbourne, running his own restaurant had been one of Bongha Kim's oldest dreams. When Bongha and his wife, Junghee Park, found a small restaurant property in the centre of Norwich, they instantly knew that Bongha's dream was about to become a reality.

The Kimchi is a casual, friendly and cosy restaurant on the first floor of an historic building on Brigg Street. It's named after the traditional Korean dish of fermented cabbage or radish, which Koreans class as one of the most important foods in their lives; just as kimchi is a staple on every Korean dining table, The Kimchi strives to become a staple in Norwich's food scene. The couple are passionate about sharing their love for the foods they grew up with, serving nothing but nostalgia and authenticity.

Bongha and Junghee are inspired by the food of their childhoods and the dishes they loved to eat when they were in South Korea. Bibimbaps, Korean Fried Chicken (aka KFC) and Korean barbecue dishes – which feature beef marinated in sweet soy sauce, or bulgogi – are the running favourites with staff and customers alike, with new dishes occasionally added to the menu. Some of their ingredients are imported from South Korea, such as chilli flakes and noodles, while most fresh ingredients are sourced locally. Chicken is very important to The Kimchi's menu and they only use the freshly prepared chicken thighs (never frozen chicken) from their local butcher.

In fact, Bongha and Jungee are so fussy about their chicken that when they initially opened the restaurant in 2019, they phoned up several Norfolk poultry farms directly to ask if they could supply The Kimchi. "Obviously they didn't deal with a small business like us themselves and I am sure they laughed at us! One of them kindly directed us to a local butcher who could source fresh chicken meat for us, and we have been with that same butcher ever since."

As the head chef and general manager respectively, Bongha and Junghee are supported by around 15 staff members who work alongside the couple to make The Kimchi the bustling restaurant that it is today. The ambitious owners are planning to open another food retail venue in 2023 and several more in the future; they are cooking up plenty of exciting ideas alongside their delicious Korean food at The Kimchi, so keep your eyes peeled for more!

KIMCHI FOR BEGINNERS

Preparation time: 20 minutes, plus 2 hours brining | Serves 10

If you've never done it before, making kimchi may seem daunting and you might not know where to begin. Actually, it is not so complicated and with this simple recipe anyone can enjoy delicious, healthy homemade kimchi without compromising on the authentic flavour.

1 Chinese cabbage (1kg)
100g coarse sea salt (not table salt)
50g sliced spring onion

For the vegetable stock

1 cabbage core, washed (see method)
2 spring onion stems, washed
50g onion
50g apple
10g dried sea kelp (optional)
10g dried shiitake mushrooms (optional)
400ml water

For the kimchi paste

60g onion
40g apple
35g garlic
15g ginger
15g white sugar
55g fish sauce
30g cooked white rice (or cooked potato)
150ml vegetable stock (see above)
35g Korean chilli flakes

Cut the cabbage into quarters lengthwise from the root, then cut each quarter into bite-size pieces. Remove and retain the core for the stock.

Place the prepared cabbage in a large bowl. Sprinkle with the coarse salt, then pour in a cup of cold water. Gently mix it through. Let the cabbage soak for 2 hours, turning it upside down every 30 minutes. To know when it's done, gently bend the white stem piece. If it bends without breaking, it's ready. Rinse the cabbage in cold water twice, then drain in a colander for 15 minutes.

While the cabbage is draining, make the vegetable stock by combining everything in a pot. Bring to the boil, then simmer over a medium heat for 20 minutes. Discard the solid ingredients, reserve 150ml of the liquid and leave it to cool down.

Tip: If you are using potato instead of rice in the kimchi paste, peel the potato and put it in the stock pot to cook while the stock simmers. Check the potato by poking it with a knife. When cooked through, take it out and set aside. This starch component (whether potato or rice) is essential for the fermentation process in making your kimchi.

Combine all the kimchi paste ingredients except the Korean chilli flakes in a blender. If you want to make vegan kimchi, simply use vegan fish sauce or Korean soup soy sauce (guk-gan-jang) which has a similar flavour profile. Blitz until smooth, then pour the paste into a large mixing bowl. Add the Korean chilli flakes and mix well.

Put the drained cabbage and sliced spring onion in the bowl, then mix well to coat them with the paste. Taste and adjust the seasoning to your liking. Kimchi, at this stage, should be spicier and saltier than you would hope for. The strong taste will subside as it ferments.

Store the kimchi in a jar, leaving some room for expansion at the top as it will expand during fermentation. Let it sit at room temperature for a day (or half a day in warm weather) and then keep in the fridge. You can eat it the same day it was made, but it is best after a few days or a week later. It will keep in the fridge for 1-2 months. Kimchi is a great side for any rice, noodle or meat dish.

BIBIMBAP (KOREAN RICE BOWL)

Preparation time: 20 minutes | Cooking time: 30 minutes | Serves 4

Literally meaning 'mixed rice with meat and assorted vegetables', bibimbap has gained popularity across the world in recent years. You can make this wholesome and healthy dish at home in less than an hour. Bibimbap can be tailored to your preferences so choose your favourite toppings, use up the vegetables in your fridge, make it vegetarian or vegan and so on.

4 portions of cooked white rice

4 eggs

200g spinach

300g beansprouts

300g courgette

½ clove of garlic, minced

300g carrot

300g mushrooms (any kind)

Salt and pepper

For the beef topping

200g minced or shredded beef

25g soy sauce

15g sugar

10g sesame oil

10g minced garlic

A pinch of black pepper

For the sauce

100g Korean chilli paste (gochujang)

15g sesame oil

15g soy sauce

10g sugar

First, marinate the minced beef in the soy sauce, sugar, sesame oil, garlic and black pepper. Now make the bibimbap sauce by combining the Korean chilli paste with the sesame oil, soy sauce and sugar in a bowl.

Next, prepare and cook the vegetables. Blanch the spinach in boiling water for 30 seconds, then drain and gently squeeze out the water. Season with a quarter teaspoon of salt and a drizzle of sesame oil. Blanch the beansprouts in boiling water for 1 minute, then drain and squeeze out the excess water. Season with a quarter teaspoon of salt, black pepper and a few drops of sesame oil.

Slice the courgette into half-moons. Heat 1 tablespoon of oil in a pan over a medium heat. Add the courgette and minced garlic with half a teaspoon of salt, then stir fry for about a minute.

Cut the carrot into thin matchsticks. Heat 1 tablespoon of oil in a pan over a medium heat and stir fry the carrot with half a teaspoon of salt for 2 minutes.

Slice the mushrooms thinly. Heat 1 tablespoon of oil in a pan over medium heat and toss the mushrooms in the oil with half a teaspoon of salt and a pinch of black pepper for 2 minutes.

Cook the marinated beef in a pan until brown, then set it aside. Cook the eggs in a frying pan until done to your liking (sunny side up).

To assemble the bibimbap, spoon the cooked and reheated rice into a large serving bowl. Arrange the vegetables on top and place the beef in the centre. Finally, add a fried egg on top. Drizzle the bibimbap sauce directly over the rice bowl or serve it on the side if preferred.

Tips:

Any other vegetables such as cabbage, bell peppers, kale, etc. can be substituted. Just lightly stir fry them with a little bit of seasoning. Any thinly sliced salad vegetables work great too. For vegetarian/vegan bibimbap, you can simply omit the beef and eggs, or replace them with tofu.

THE KINGS OF NORFOLK

The Kings Arms Fleggburgh is a must-visit for any food lover in Norfolk
thanks to the team's passionate approach to food, drink and beautiful surroundings
to enjoy it all in.

Set in the country village of Fleggburgh, this stunning destination restaurant with rooms and a pub has been open for over a decade with owner Mark Dixon at the helm. Mark is Norfolk born and bred, comes from a farming family, and is a classically trained chef; food has always been a very important part of his life and he achieved his dream of owning a restaurant when he opened The Kings Arms Fleggburgh in 2013. Mark and his talented team have since transformed the former boozer into one of the finest foodie hotspots in Norfolk, which now boasts two AA Rosettes.

The Kings Arms Fleggburgh opens for breakfast, lunch and dinner with enticing options including the seven-course tasting menu alongside favourites such as chargrilled steak and chips. They make everything in-house daily, from the breads to the sorbets, and cater for all tastes with daily changing dishes. Mark's extensive experience brings a level of refinement and creativity to the kitchen, as he has formerly worked in restaurants across the globe, from Sky Tower restaurant in New Zealand to Simon Rogan's Cumbrian L'Enclume. Shortly before taking on The Kings Arms Fleggburgh, he was crowned Norfolk Chef of the Year and has competed internationally in the likes of Chaine des Rotisseurs at Le Cordon Bleu London and at the Royal Academy of Culinary Arts.

Despite his well-travelled background, there really is no place like home for Mark and the rural setting that surrounds his pub and restaurant informs every dish on the menu. Seasonality and Norfolk's very best produce are key features at The Kings Arms Fleggburgh, from locally reared meat to fresh fish deliveries. They even have a country garden producing some of their own herbs, edible flowers, fruit, and vegetables which are picked daily by the team of chefs.

In addition to the award-winning restaurant, The Kings Arms Fleggburgh has three self-contained garden rooms and four boutique bedrooms within the main building for guests to stay overnight. Their most recent addition, The Barn, is a cosy converted bar serving Spanish tapas alongside cocktails, wines, and local beers, adding yet another string to the bow of this hugely successful dining destination nestled in the Norfolk countryside.

NORFOLK WOOD PIGEON

Preparation time: 20-30 minutes | Cooking time: 30-40 minutes | Serves 4

This delicate dish combines rich pigeon breast with an earthy truffle-spiked mushroom risotto, enhanced with confit egg yolk, crispy pancetta and fresh watercress. It's bound to impress your dinner guests but easier to make than you might think!

450g chestnut mushrooms

15g butter

Pinch of sea salt and black pepper

300g arborio risotto rice

1 litre chicken stock

200ml white wine

2-3 tbsp grated parmesan

3 tsp white truffle oil

570ml (1 pint) vegetable oil

4 free-range eggs

8 slices of pancetta

4 pigeon breasts

Handful of baby watercress

100ml red wine jus, to serve

First, chop the mushrooms into bite-size pieces about 0.5cm square. Melt the butter in a sauté pan over a medium heat, then add the mushroom. Sprinkle with salt and pepper, then sauté for 2-3 minutes until the mushrooms are soft.

Pour the rice into the pan and gently stir so the rice is spread throughout the mushrooms and coated in butter. Now gradually add a ladle of chicken stock. Stir the mushrooms and rice gently until they have absorbed the stock and you can't see any liquid. Continue adding ladles of stock to the pan, stirring constantly and waiting until it has been absorbed each time, until you've added 500ml.

Add the white wine to the pan and stir until it has been absorbed. Add the remaining stock a ladle at a time, again stirring gently until it has been absorbed. After each ladle, test the rice to see if it's cooked the way you like it, from al dente to soft. If it's not soft enough, stir in another ladle of stock.

Stir in the grated parmesan and truffle oil to finish the risotto, then take the pan off the heat and leave it for 2 minutes, allowing the mushrooms and rice to absorb all the different flavours.

Meanwhile, pour the vegetable oil into a deep pan and warm it to 58°c. Carefully separate the eggs and place the yolks into the warm oil. Once all the yolks are in, take the pan off the heat and let it sit undisturbed until needed. Grill the pancetta on a tray until crispy and golden, then place on paper towels to absorb the grease and help it stay crispy.

To cook the pigeon, heat a knob of butter and a dash of oil in a clean pan. Once the butter starts to turn golden, add the pigeon breasts and lower the heat. Once golden, turn them over and cook for a further minute, then leave to rest in the pan off the heat for 4 minutes somewhere warm.

Once you are ready to serve, spoon the risotto into warm bowls, slice each pigeon breast into 3 or 4 pieces and place these on top, then carefully transfer the confit egg yolks from the oil to the bowls. Garnish with the pancetta, watercress, and a spoonful of the red wine jus over the pigeon. Enjoy!

PAN SEARED SEA BREAM AND BROWN SHRIMPS

Preparation time: 15-20 minutes | Cooking time: 25-30 minutes | Serves 4

This indulgent seafood dish pairs sea bream with brown shrimps, served among
the bright and vibrant flavours of a pea, leek and white wine fricassee.

For the pea, leek and white wine fricassee

50g butter

1 banana shallot, diced

1 leek, washed, halved and thinly sliced

1 bay leaf

100ml white wine

100ml fish stock

100ml cream

100g fresh peas

50g sugar snap peas, sliced lengthways

1 lemon, juiced

Salt and pepper

50ml lovage oil

For the bream

4 large sea bream fillets

100g brown shrimps

Selection of micro herbs

20 crispy potatoes, blanched and fried
in butter

60g lovage and parsley emulsion

For the pea, leek and white wine fricassee

Add the butter, shallots, leeks and bay leaf to a thick-bottomed, heavy saucepan on a medium heat.
Lightly sweat just until soft.

Turn up the heat a little, then add the white wine and reduce. Once reduced, add the remaining
ingredients except the oil, then bring to the boil and keep warm.

Just before serving, add the lovage oil to split the sauce.

For the bream

In a frying pan, heat a little drizzle of olive oil. Once hot, add the fish to the pan (skin side down).
Lower the heat and cook until golden, then flip over. Turn the pan off immediately to let the fish
keep cooking gently. Add the shrimps on top of the fish to warm, then garnish with herbs.

To plate, spoon the vegetables and all the sauce into a deep bowl. Garnish the edges of the bowl
with the crispy potatoes, then place the fish on top with the emulsion on the side.

RED DEER

Preparation time: 1 hour | Cooking time: 40 minutes | Serves 4

A warming wintery delight, this dish is served with dauphinoise potatoes, creamed savoy cabbage,
salsify roasted with Douglas fir oil, celeriac purée and Port jus. It's sophisticated yet simple enough for
anyone to make at home: the perfect recipe to try in a cosy kitchen on a cold winter weekend.

4 x 150g red deer loins

Knob of salted butter

Rapeseed oil

4 sticks of salsify

4 baby beetroot, peeled and halved

1 cup of Port jus, heated

Panko breadcrumbs

Douglas fir oil

Salt and pepper

For the dauphinoise potatoes

500ml double cream

500ml milk

3 cloves of garlic, peeled

8 large King Edward potatoes

100g grated gruyere cheese

For the celeriac purée

200g celeriac, diced

20g butter

100ml whole milk

50ml double cream

For the creamed savoy cabbage

50g butter

8 slices of pancetta

1 savoy cabbage, very thinly shredded

50ml cider

100g double cream

For the dauphinoise potatoes

Preheat the oven to 190°c/170°c fan/gas mark 5. Simmer the double cream, milk and garlic cloves in a large saucepan. Slice the potatoes very finely (3-4mm) and simmer them in the cream mixture for 3 minutes until just cooked. Stir gently to separate and stop them catching on the bottom of the pan.

Using a slotted spoon, transfer the potatoes to a wide shallow ovenproof dish, forming a layer about 5cm deep. Pour over just enough infused cream (discarding the garlic) to seep through the potato and leave a little moisture on the surface. Scatter the grated gruyere on top, then bake in the preheated oven for 30 minutes until the potatoes are soft. Increase the heat for a final 5 minutes if the top hasn't browned enough.

For the celeriac purée

In a large saucepan on a medium heat, soften the celeriac in the butter for 5 minutes covered with a lid. Add the milk and cream, season with salt and pepper, then cook on a low heat for 10 minutes until the celeriac is completely soft. Use a slotted spoon to transfer the celeriac to a food processor with a little of the hot milk. Blend to a smooth purée, starting on a low speed and building up to full power. Never fill your blender over halfway with hot liquid.

For the creamed savoy cabbage

Heat a pan, add the butter and fry the pancetta until it has a little colour. Stir in the shredded cabbage and cook until softened, then add the cider and heat until reduced. Pour in the cream, then season with salt and pepper to taste.

To assemble the dish

To cook the red deer, preheat the oven to 180°c/gas mark 4. Seal the loins in a hot frying pan with a little butter and rapeseed oil until golden brown all over. Add the salsify and baby beetroot to the pan, then transfer it to the oven and cook for 8 minutes. This will result in medium rare meat, so cook longer for medium to well done. Remove the pan from the oven and rest the loins on a wire rack for 5-8 minutes. Meanwhile, scatter the salsify with panko breadcrumbs and drizzle with Douglas fir oil, then place back into oven until golden brown. Spoon the celeriac purée onto your plates, add some creamed cabbage and place two nice slices of red deer on each one. Add the crispy salsify, drizzle the dish with warmed Port jus and serve with dauphinoise potatoes on the side.

FOOD FIT FOR A KING

Located in the quiet and pretty village of Bawburgh,
The Kings Head is an award-winning 17th century freehouse pub,
restaurant and B&B, steeped in history and full of character.

For 40 years, The Kings Head has been under the stewardship of The Wimmer Family, who bought the 17th century pub in 1983 after falling in love with the history, peaceful location and the onsite squash courts. Initially run as a sporting club but now functioning as a pub, restaurant and B&B, The Kings Head welcomes scores of customers from all over Norfolk for a refreshing drink and a bite to eat.

Anton Wimmer's passion for great food and wine resulted in The Kings Head becoming one of the original pioneers of gastropub dining. Now highly respected as one of the top gastropubs in Norfolk, with a wealth of awards under their belt including two AA rosettes, the quaint countryside pub has a creative and comprehensive menu. With a cosy bar, spacious main restaurant, and stylish private dining room, plus an adaptable al fresco area complete with a louvre roof and a sunny patio garden, there is a space for all in the atmosphere of your choice.

Before even tucking into the food, it's clear that the menus are firmly rooted in local markets. The talented team prepare their dishes with the freshest ingredients, evident in their monthly-changing seasonal menu packed with hearty pub classics. Alongside this runs a weekly changing '48.5 mile' special menu of finer dining dishes, all created to showcase the incredible produce available in the radius of Bawburgh, including from 'Pam's Garden', just around the corner where produce and herbs are freshly grown specifically for The Kings Head. Their 'pie of the day' is encased with the most incredible buttery pastry and is not to be missed – a firm customer favourite. You could also sample the staff favourite dessert of banana and passionfruit baked Alaska – zesty and delicious.

In 2015, this countryside pub became a B&B with the addition of six meticulously designed boutique rooms, all named after key stalwarts of their history. Now offering an enviable welcome and delicious dining, as well as a relaxing and tranquil place to rest your head overnight, The Kings Head is a home away from home. Anton's own words sum up The Kings Head perfectly: "We want to have one of the warmest welcomes in Norfolk, so that you feel at ease while you are with us, whether that is for a quick bite to eat, sumptuous dinner or a relaxing night away."

NORFOLK STRAWBERRY AND WHITE CHOCOLATE DOME

Preparation time: 5 hours 30 minutes | Cooking time: 1 hour | Serves 12

There is nothing better than strawberries and white chocolate together. A silky smooth and indulgent white chocolate cremeux tops a delicious strawberry parfait to give you a refreshingly sweet treat! Locally sourced strawberries are incredible, but you can of course use any strawberries depending on the seasons.

For the strawberry purée
900g strawberries
180g caster sugar
1 lemon, juiced

For the parfait
100g egg yolk
50ml water
455ml double cream

For the white chocolate cremeux
325g white chocolate, chopped into small pieces
150g mascarpone

For the jelly
1.5 gelatine leaves, soaked in water

To serve
Handful of mini meringues

Special Equipment
Silicone dome moulds (one for parfait and one for the white chocolate domes)
A sugar thermometer

For the strawberry purée
Top and chop 750g of the strawberries and add to a blender with 2 tablespoons of sugar and the lemon juice. Blitz until a smooth purée is formed. Place to the side.

For the parfait
Place the egg yolk in a mixer and whisk until doubled in size. Add 150g of the sugar to a pan with the water. Bring the sugar and water to a boil until they reach 115°c. Slowly pour this over the egg yolks and whisk until cooled. Then, add 500g of the strawberry purée and whisk until combined. In another bowl, whisk 300ml of the double cream until it starts to stiffen and then fold the cream through the strawberry mixture. Pour the parfait into moulds and set in the freezer for 4-5 hours.

For the white chocolate cremeux
In a separate pan, bring the remaining double cream to the boil, remove from the stove, and pour over 225g of the chopped white chocolate. Whisk gently until combined.
Soften the mascarpone in a bowl, add this to the chocolate mixture and whisk together. Place the cremeux in a piping bag and pop in the fridge to set slightly for 3-4 hours.

For the white chocolate dome
Chop the remaining white chocolate into small pieces and melt gently in a bowl over a lightly simmering pan of water (ensure the bowl doesn't touch the water). When melted, pour into the moulds, coat them, and pour out any excess. Pop in the freezer until needed.

For the jelly
Combine the remaining strawberry purée, water and 1 tablespoon of caster sugar in a pan and bring to a gentle boil for a few minutes. Then, add the gelatine leaves and mix until dissolved. Remove from the boil and pour into a container. Cut into cubes using a hot knife when cool.

For the strawberry salsa
Dice the remaining strawberries, sprinkle with icing sugar, and add a splash of water.

To serve
Gently remove each white chocolate dome from the mould and pipe the cremeux into the dome. Remove the parfait from the mould and place flat side up on the plate. Place the filled domes on top of the strawberry parfait. Decorate around the dome with chopped strawberries, strawberry salsa, mini meringues, and strawberry jelly cubes.

FOR THE LOVE OF LOCAL

Zena, the host of Norwich Food & Drink Walking Tours, is a seasoned foodie who loves to rave about all the magnificent produce Norfolk has on its doorstep.

Norwich Food & Drink Walking Tours began with a trip abroad when founder Zena booked a food tour in Lisbon. She wondered why nothing like that existed in her hometown of Norwich and so the idea for her new venture was born.

Although Norwich may not be the first place that comes to mind when thinking of tourist hotspots, Norfolk is a popular county to visit and the city itself boasts over 500 food businesses, plus the range of produce to be found just on the doorstep is incredible. Norwich has the biggest open air market in the UK with dozens of food stalls, and the hundreds of independent eateries are nestled between medieval churches, cobbled streets, a bustling high street and a winding river: plenty of picture-perfect stops for a bite to eat or your favourite tipple.

To Zena, it was obvious that all this had to be celebrated with bespoke and group food tour options, allowing everyone to sample some of the delights Norwich has on offer. After experiencing many food tours around the globe, Zena wanted hers to be all about the food with no one walking away hungry. They are jam packed with flavour, facts, and hidden gems to explore – it's all about having fun and making the tour a unique experience, thanks to lots of local knowledge, a touch of the city's history, and a splash of booze (local of course)!

The most popular part of the tour is always Norwich's market; people are amazed at what's on offer there as Zena takes them on a snaking path through the stalls, making sure nothing is missed, which also includes several stops for tasters. After that, the tour involves a walk around the city taking in the historic Elm Hill, part of the Lanes including an independent pub or bar, a sit down stop or two starter-sized tasters, and a hot drink and cake to bring the tour to a satisfying end.

Zena offers bespoke tours for two to four people along with group bookings. They usually run on Tuesdays, Wednesdays or Thursdays from 11am as Zena also runs Lodge Farm Holiday Barns where there are three holiday homes to manage, along with food writing, blogging and the occasional cookery class. Tours usually last about three hours. Full details can be found on www.lovenorwichfood.co.uk and you must pre-book, so be sure to check it out!

NORFOLK GOAT'S CHEESE WHIP WITH DATE CRACKERS AND BEETROOT COULIS

Preparation time: 40-45 minutes | Cooking time: 15 minutes | Serves 3-4 as a starter or light lunch

I wanted to use not only foraged ingredients from my garden (the nettles, blackberries, and wild garlic) but also local produce, so 85-90% of the ingredients in this recipe are sold at Blofield Farm Shop, including the Norfolk White Lady goat's cheese and the Nortons Dairy cream cheese.

For the goat's cheese whip

125g Norfolk White Lady goat's cheese
(from Willow Farm)

75g cream cheese

2-3 wild garlic leaves (or ½ clove of
garlic + 1 tsp chopped fresh parsley)

½ tsp chopped capers or gherkins

½ tsp brine from the capers or gherkins

1 tsp fresh lemon juice

¼ tsp fresh lemon zest

A generous amount of black pepper

For the date crackers

75g chopped nuts (walnuts and
almonds)

30g spelt flour
(or brown rice/buckwheat flour)

30g dried dates, finely chopped

20ml melted coconut oil

1 tsp each black and white sesame seeds

½ tbsp maple syrup, honey, date syrup
or agave

For the beetroot coulis

65g cooked beetroot

65g foraged blackberries

A handful of stinging nettle tops

1 tsp lemon juice

½ tsp garam masala

½ tsp ground turmeric

For the goat's cheese whip

Simply blend all the ingredients together in a processor or crush and mix them in a bowl with a fork.

For the date crackers

Mix all the ingredients together in a bowl until thoroughly combined. I like to firm up the dough by leaving it to rest in the fridge for 20 minutes or more, rolled up like a sausage in cling film.

You can now slice the chilled log of dough into thin rounds, or I used a mini scone cutter to cut out the crackers from thinly rolled dough. It is very pliable and can be moulded by hand into tart cases too or rolled into balls and pressed into patties with damp hands.

Place the crackers on a greased baking sheet and bake in a preheated oven at 160°c for 12-15 minutes. Leave to cool.

For the beetroot coulis

Simply blend the ingredients together in a processor or whizz with a hand blender until smooth. For extra silkiness, pass the coulis through a sieve.

To serve

You can serve this dish in two ways, either with a spoonful of goat's cheese whip and beetroot coulis in a ramekin with a few crackers to scoop them up, or as a plated starter.

For the latter, place a smooth quenelle of the goat's cheese whip in the centre, arrange 3 crackers around that, then drizzle with the beetroot coulis. Garnish with some micro herbs or edible flowers for the finishing touch.

You could also turn this dish into canapés by making the crackers smaller and topping them with teaspoons of the whip and coulis. Enjoy!

COCKTAILS MADE MINDFULLY

Did you know the average Espresso Martini contains more sugar than a can of coke? Mindful Mixology create bottled cocktails made with significantly less sugar, using small, local, and independent brands. Their cocktails are all vegan-friendly, come in plastic-free packaging and their eye-catching label designs are a nod to their donation of 5% of profits to the Music Venues Trust, supporting grassroots independent venues across the UK.

After becoming ill in 2020 and having to cut out dairy, gluten and sugar from her diet, Danni, founder of Mindful Mixology, noticed a gap in the market for cocktails that were made with less sugar and with transparent labelling. Hence the creation of Mindful Mixology, where cocktails are made, well, more mindfully!

Danni is passionate about working with small and independent brands, using locally sourced ingredients where she can, working directly with companies that have a strong sustainability ethos. The Lychee Martini and Raspberry and Elderflower Collins both contain vermouth from In The Loop, based in Sussex, that uses leftover base wine from a local winery and local ingredients to create a delicious, award-winning vermouth, made in a closed-loop system.

The Salted Coconut Espresso Martini is still the firm favourite of all the Mindful Mixology cocktails - made with Norfolk Rum's coconut liqueur and Fairtrade coffee that Danni brews herself, with a dash of vanilla, coconut blossom, coffee liqueur and sea salt. The result is a smooth, delicious cocktail that is perfect for all seasons. In keeping with the company's ethos, the cocktail uses organic coconut blossom in place of sugar syrup and has 70% less sugar than the average Espresso Martini.

Danni's creations have attracted lots of positive attention, been featured in The Metro and The Guardian, and have even been promoted by Davina McCall who called them "the cutest little cocktail in a bottle." Alongside the business being the winner of five Great Taste awards and a "Free From" award sponsored by Tesco, the Lychee Martini won the Great Taste 3-star award in 2022, an award reserved for just 1-2% of all international entrants.

Danni has worked all positions in the business, from website to packaging, PR and of course recipe development and manufacturing. She has since opened a bar with business partner and friend Michelle, with Mindful Mixology set to move into a bigger kitchen in Salle, where they can focus on a new range of cocktails perfect for on-trade. Looking to the future, the brand is due to release a new range of cocktails in bulk for on-trade. Available in handy refillable containers, it means bars and restaurants can reduce their waste and save money at the same time. A new range of 100ml serves, perfect for farm shops and delis, are due to launch in time for Christmas 2023.

APPLE OF MY EYE

Preparation time: 20 minutes | Cooking time: 15 minutes | Serves 1

In Norfolk, I had my first taste of stewed apples, cooked fresh from the garden. I've created a recipe inspired by Norfolk summers, adding elderflower and apple to a simple gin, lemon, and sugar base. You can make the apple purée in advance and adapt seasonally with rhubarb or blackberries for an equally delicious result.

For the apple purée

500g of your favourite apples, peeled, cored, and quartered

50g organic raw caster sugar

50ml water

For the cocktail

50ml Norfolk Gin

25ml lemon juice

20ml wild elderflower cordial

2 tsp apple purée

Splash of soda water

Organic agave syrup (optional)

For the apple purée

Place the apples (we love a Cox's or a Golden Noble) in a medium pan and cover with the raw caster sugar and 2-3 tablespoons of water.

Cover the pan and cook on a medium heat. When it starts to boil, cook for 5 minutes, stirring halfway through.

The apples will start to dissolve. At this stage add about 50ml of water and stir vigorously until you have a purée. You can also save time by popping it in a blender once cooled.

Add sugar or water to your taste, and to get the desired consistency.

Keep in your fridge for up to one week or freeze. This purée can be used for future cocktails, but also makes a great base for crumbles, desserts or savoury dishes.

For the cocktail

In a cocktail shaker (or a jam jar with a lid) add the gin, freshly squeezed lemon juice, elderflower cordial (we like to use Norfolk Cordial) and apple purée.

Add a scoop of ice to the shaker, close it and shake vigorously until a layer of condensation has formed.

In a chunky glass add a scoop of fresh ice cubes.

Strain your cocktail over the ice. You don't want clumps of the purée or apple in there. Top with a splash of soda water.

To serve

Garnish with an apple fan or a sprig of garden mint.

Top Tip

If the cocktail tastes too sweet, add a drop more lemon juice. If it's too sour, add 5ml of organic agave syrup or a drop more elderflower cordial.

MORE THAN CUTTING THE MUSTARD

The only single estate mustard manufacturer in Europe, Montys Mustards and Chutneys produces Norfolk's finest condiments to liven up any meal with bags of local flavour.

Montys Mustards and Chutneys was established in 2017 to coincide with Edward Savage's return to the family business, Essence Foods, which originally produced jams and marmalade but progressed over the years to become an umbrella brand for a wide range of products. It was also partly prompted by Colman's moving their UK production out of Norfolk after 150 years of making mustard in the county. More than simply adding a product to their range, Ed and his family wanted to bring mustard back home after realising how much would be lost: not just jobs but heritage too.

With a vision to reconnect with this history and keep mustard current, Montys began with traditional flavours using local ingredients – Norfolk ales, horseradish, honey – and gradually expanded to the 21 different mustards and chutneys they have today. Whether you're making a toastie or whipping up a glamorous evening meal, Montys products can give it that little lift with their clever twists on classic flavours: try the Bloody Mary Relish with your cooked breakfast, date-based Norfolk Pickle on your cheeseboard, or honey and cinnamon mustard in pretty much anything.

"A bit of boldness and bravery in the kitchen makes a world of difference," says Edward of the Montys philosophy. "When you're looking for that extra depth of flavour and not quite sure what a dish needs, try a proper mustard and see where the experimentation takes you." The family-run business is so passionate about true Norfolk mustard that they even grow their own, bringing the very seeds of their signature product in-house from planting to harvest.

Luckily for those of us outside mustard's historical home, you can find Montys online, in stockists around the country, and at food festivals and shows, of which the team try to get round as many as possible. There's also a shop and café on site for visitors to try before they buy, plus many supporters in the surrounding area such as The Crown Hotel at Wells who have long been fans of Montys products. Over the years they have won countless awards both nationally and internationally, balancing sustainable growth with the goal of reaching as many customers as they can – even as far flung as the UAE where they are now stocked in supermarkets.

"We just want people to take time and pleasure in the food they're eating," says Edward, "and with the local ingredients, heritage and expertise that goes into our mustards and chutneys, we hope Montys is a part of that enjoyment for all our customers."

ULTIMATE FRIDGE RAID TOASTIE

Preparation time: 30 minutes | Cooking time: 20 minutes | Serves 1 (the most important person: YOU!)

This was created after a long weekend show during the autumn food festival season. Having finished unloading from the day before, a proper fridge raid was the best way to replenish our energy reserves. This recipe is great at using up odd jars of mustard in the fridge door, with a little bit of indulgence from the Brie-style Copys Cloud cheese to comfort the soul.

1 tsp Montys Bandersnatch Mustard

1 clove of garlic, finely chopped

½ tsp soy sauce

A pinch of black pepper

10ml rapeseed oil

1 chicken breast

2 tbsp mayonnaise

2 tsp Montys Honey and Cinnamon Mustard

2 tsp finely chopped fresh parsley

1 clove of garlic, minced

Salt and pepper, to taste

Softened butter, for the bread

2 slices of white sourdough bread

4 slices of Mrs Temple's Copys Cloud (a Brie-style Norfolk cheese)

1 fresh, crispy lettuce leaf (iceberg lettuce is our favourite)

1 beef tomato, sliced

First, make a marinade by whisking the Montys Bandersnatch Mustard, garlic, soy sauce and black pepper together in a bowl. Whisking constantly, add the rapeseed oil in a constant stream to combine the mixture, then add the chicken breast and turn until completely coated in the marinade. Let this sit at room temperature, covered, for 30 minutes or up to 4 hours in the fridge. Meanwhile, make the dressing. Mix the mayonnaise, Montys Honey and Cinnamon Mustard, fresh parsley, and minced garlic together in a bowl. If you want to try something a bit different, use lovage instead of the parsley for a savoury flavour not unlike celery, but either will be delicious. Season this dressing with salt and pepper to taste. Butter one side of each slice of bread ready for your toastie.

Once you've waited long enough for the chicken, put a pan on a medium-high heat and lightly coat the base with oil. Cook the marinated chicken in the hot pan for 8-10 minutes, turning it over halfway through, until the outside has a nice char and the internal temperature reaches 75°c. This can also be done on a barbecue if the weather is right! Once cooked, set the chicken aside to rest. While the chicken rests, place the bread buttered side down into the same pan and toast until golden brown. When toasted, you are ready to start assembling the sandwich. Take a slice of bread and spread the untoasted side with half your honey mustard dressing. Slice and add the chicken, then cover with the slices of Copys Cloud cheese. If you like, this can now be grilled to melt the cheese for extra indulgence! Add the lettuce and tomato, spread the other slice of bread with the remaining honey mustard dressing, then pop this on top and you're ready to enjoy a feast! If it's a nice sunny day and the mood is right, this toastie is great with a glass of chilled Burn Valley Vineyard Solaris.

TASTE SENSATIONS AND CELEBRATIONS

A friendly, tucked away, neighbourhood treat, The Mulberry is a discreet and welcoming business that focuses on delivering the best food from a varied yet delightful menu.

An intimate yet welcoming atmosphere greets you from the moment you enter the gorgeous, curved doors of The Mulberry in Thetford. The building dates back to the 1800s when the Thetford & Watton Times of 1886 states it to be a "baker's shop with a first-class oven" with the census of 1861 listing the occupant as a baker. Over the years, the building has been extended and adapted, combining the charm of an older building with modern day comforts; high ceilings and space between tables allowing an airy feel even on a warm evening.

Opened by the current owners in 2010, the restaurant is relaxed and pleasantly informal while offering high quality Mediterranean and English style food using traditional methods and the finest locally sourced produce, such as Pure Norfolk Honey produced by the Sigleys, less than a quarter of a mile down the road, and Jolly Asparagus grown at Roudham Farm, seven and a half miles away. Menus change frequently, adapting to both seasonal availability and to suit the ever-increasing number of clients who have discovered this little gem of a restaurant, which sits just on the edge of the centre of Thetford. The Mulberry is a discreet, relaxed, and friendly oasis with a walled garden, situated on the corner of Cage Lane and Raymond Street, just a few paces from several of the free car parks in town.

The food of The Mulberry is the focus, when only the best will do. This is proven by the fine flavours and taste sensations which end up on your plate; nothing pretentious, just simple cooked food prepared from the finest ingredients. The chef produces his own stocks and sauces, butchers his own meat to find the choicest cuts, and prepares all the fresh fish and seafood used in the dishes. After 13 years, The Mulberry is a part of the community, celebrating every occasion including engagements, wedding receptions, anniversaries, birthdays, reunions and even being used to film episodes of Location, Location, Location, Long Lost Family and a menu reveal for Come Dine With Me! The reviews online say it all; full of praise for the food, ambience, and service with the clientele, both local and from further afield, growing every year.

JUMBO PRAWN BRUSCHETTA

Preparation time: 30 minutes | Cooking time: 50-60 minutes for the stock, 10 minutes for the prawns | Serves 4

At The Mulberry, all the stocks and sauces are made from scratch, often using leftover bones or, in this case, lobster shells. If you can make your own stock, you will really taste the difference and the good thing is you can freeze it too!

2 tbsp extra virgin olive oil, plus a drizzle for serving

1 large onion, peeled and chopped

2 cloves of garlic, plus 1 clove for ciabatta and 1 tsp for prawns, chopped

2 sticks of celery, chopped

2 small leeks, chopped

3 lobster bodies (shells only), chopped

140ml brandy

1 tbsp tomato paste

2 tsp tarragon

280ml white wine

3 litres water

Salt to taste

12 prawns, peeled and de-veined

4 prawns, head and shell on

1 tbsp cannellini beans

1 tbsp chopped tomatoes or cherry tomatoes

2 fresh basil leaves, thinly sliced

4 ciabatta slices, rubbed with garlic and grilled

2 knobs of butter

Lemon zest to serve

For the stock

Heat the olive oil in a large stock pot and sauté the onion, garlic, celery and leeks with the chopped lobster bodies until they change colour from blue to red.

Add the brandy to the pot and flame (use a long handled lighter and mind your eyebrows!).

Add the tomato paste and tarragon, then stir well.

Add the white wine, put the lid on the pot and steam for 10 minutes.

Remove the lid and add the water. Bring the stock up to a simmer and cook for 30 minutes. Add salt to taste and strain.

For the prawns

Heat some olive oil in a large frying pan, then add the teaspoon of chopped garlic and the prawns.

As they start to change colour, add the cannellini beans, tomatoes, and basil.

Add 6 tablespoons of the stock to coat the prawns.

Add the butter to finish.

To serve

Assemble the toast, prawns, and sauce with the head-and-shell-on prawns on the top, a drizzle of extra virgin olive oil, lemon zest and basil leaf. An extra nice touch is to serve with a finger bowl on the side.

Optional extras

Courgette (cooked with prawns), spinach (added to prawns with the stock) or hummus spread on the ciabatta.

A TASTE OF INDIA

Namaste Village, a vibrant and heartwarming restaurant in Norwich, was born from a dream to bring purely vegetarian, authentic Indian cuisine to the UK.

Founded in 2010 by Vijay Jetani, Urmila Jetani and Dalsukh Jetani as Namaste India, the restaurant was small, yet it steadily grew and evolved. In 2016, Ketan Vaghasiya joined the team, leading to the birth of Namaste Village, a high-end, traditional Indian restaurant dedicated exclusively to vegetarian and vegan food. Housed in a former church school, the restaurant beautifully combines history and Indian traditions.

Namaste Village's team pride themselves on the diversity and richness of Indian cuisine, which reflects the nation's people, culture, and heritage. From the spice fairs in the north to the bountiful flavours of the south, from the rich Mughlai delicacies to the exotic tastes of the east and west, their menu celebrates the full spectrum of Indian flavours.

However, beyond the delectable dishes lies the true essence of Indian sentiment – a shared experience of culture. As guests from all walks of life and cultures converge in this restaurant, they leave their differences at the door, coming together to dine, drink, and engage in meaningful conversations. The act of breaking naan bread together fosters relationships and celebrates a shared love for food and each other. This spirit of togetherness and celebration is deeply ingrained in Namaste Village's Indian heritage, and they carry it forward with pride.

A key factor in the restaurant's success has been the unwavering support and generosity of the Norfolk community: "Norwich welcomed us with open arms, and we are forever grateful for the familiar faces and warm smiles that grace our doors," the team explains. Thanks to this support, Namaste Village has expanded to Cambridge and London, with a vision of reaching a global audience.

Today, Namaste Village stands at the forefront of the plant-based cuisine revolution, redefining the dining experience with high-quality meat substitutes that have won the hearts of both meat-eaters and vegans alike. Their dedication to culinary excellence and innovation has led them to create mock meat dishes that are so remarkably delicious and satisfying that even the most devoted meat-lovers have become ardent fans of their vegan and vegetarian food.

Namaste Village is more than just a restaurant; it is a celebration of Indian culture, a fusion of flavours, and a gathering place for a diverse community. From the team at Namaste Village themselves: "as we continue this culinary journey, we carry the warmth of Norfolk's love with us, and we look forward to sharing the true, pure, and authentic taste of India with the world. Thank you, dear fellow Norfolk, for making Namaste Village a cherished part of your lives and inspiring us to reach new heights on our culinary expedition."

SAAG PANEER

Preparation time: 5 minutes | Cooking time: 30 minutes | Serves 2

Saag Paneer is a popular North Indian curry made with spinach and accompanied by Indian cottage cheese (paneer). This specially curated recipe is designed for those with limited experience in Indian cooking but who have a passion for exploring Indian cuisine. For a vegan twist, feel free to substitute paneer with tofu or potato. Recipe by: Chef Urmila Jetani, curated by: Shreya Dubey.

150g fresh spinach

2 medium tomatoes

1 tbsp oil

½ tsp cumin seeds

½ tsp cloves

½ tsp cinnamon

½ tsp asafoetida (Hing)

1 tbsp ginger and green chilli paste

½ tsp salt

½ tsp ground cumin

100g paneer, cubed

Lemon juice to taste

Begin by thoroughly washing the spinach and tomatoes, then chop them both finely.

In a medium-sized saucepan, heat the oil over moderate heat. Add the cumin seeds, cloves, and cinnamon, and let them sizzle. Stir in the asafoetida, ginger and green chilli paste, salt, ground cumin, and the chopped tomatoes and spinach.

Allow the mixture to cook for approximately 10-15 minutes, or until the ingredients are tender. Once cooked, blend the mixture using a blender.

Add the mixture back into the pan and stir well. Add 2 tablespoons of water and cover the pan, lower the flame, and let it cook for 10 minutes.

In a separate pan, heat a little more oil over a medium heat and shallow fry the paneer cubes until they turn a golden-brown colour. It's important to note that frying the paneer is optional. You can also use raw paneer cubes without frying.

Incorporate the cubed paneer into the blended mixture. If desired, add a dash of lemon juice.

To add a delightful finishing touch, garnish the dish with fresh coriander leaves and a tablespoon of cream.

Notes to keep in mind:

Take care not to overcook the spinach as it can darken the dish. Cook it until it is tender and retains its vibrant green colour.

For a zero-compromise vegan version of the dish, replace the paneer with boiled potatoes or pan-fried tofu.

THE LOVE OF ALL THINGS BREAD

The Old Store was born from one specific feeling – the love of making and eating bread. It resulted in the opening of a vibrant micro-bakery and coffee shop that serves delicious things in and on bread, as well as coffee, smoothies, fresh juices and brunch cocktails.

The Old Store was developed with a concept that embraces brunch culture. What's better than starting your day off with an excellent cup of coffee and a healthy, hearty breakfast in a vibrant, relaxed atmosphere? The best English Breakfast you've tried, featuring their signature duck fat hash brown, the original Old S'muffin or the fluffy buttermilk pancakes for those with a sweet tooth are just some of the standout dishes you can sample. It won't be easy to choose!

For years, the owners, Aga and Lewis Kings, had run a successful fine dining restaurant, The Old Bank. Following its success, they decided to expand their portfolio when The Old Store's current site, the old village store and post office, came on the market. This is when Aga's sister, Ania Wadolowska, was brought on board to run it. Aga and Lewis' vision, combined with Ania's experience running busy coffee shops, together with the incredible skill of head chef Chris Mann and his team, made The Old Store what it is today.

What makes The Old Store special is that everything served is prepared on the premises using the best seasonal and, whenever possible, locally sourced produce. The Old Store works closely with the incredible Norfolk Coffee Company and they're proud to showcase their coffee in-house. The menu is focused and original, based on the quality of the ingredients used, such as the smoked salmon from the Staithe Smokehouse, in Brancaster Staithe.

In October 2022, The Old Store came third in the incredibly prestigious Tiptree World Bread Awards in the most coveted Authentic Sourdough category. The team are proud to be able to sell the third best loaf in the United Kingdom, which is at the heart of their success.

The Old Store is lucky to employ an exceptional group of passionate, friendly and hardworking people, which is the most important ingredient in the recipe for The Old Store's success. The bakery's atmosphere is vibrant and bustling, where upbeat music and bright colours help to create a buzz, making the place just as it was meant to be. Smiley and friendly service instantly makes you feel welcome, inviting you back again and again.

BUTTERMILK PANCAKES

Preparation time: 5 minutes | Cooking time: 5-6 minutes | Makes 12 pancakes

The fluffiest buttermilk pancakes you ever tasted.

275g plain flour
25g sugar
½ tsp bicarbonate of soda
2 tsp baking powder
½ tsp salt
500ml buttermilk
40g butter, melted
1 egg
1 tsp vanilla essence

In a large bowl, sift all the dry ingredients together.

In a separate bowl, whisk all the wet ingredients together until thoroughly mixed.

Combine the wet and dry ingredients and whisk to ensure no lumps remain.

Heat a non-stick pan on a medium heat. When it reaches a high temperature, start spooning in the pancake batter. You'll want 4-5 heaped tablespoons per pancake, but you can always adjust this depending on how big you like them.

Cook for 2-3 minutes on each side.

Serve with toppings of your choice!

At The Old Store we like the sweet and savoury combination of buttermilk fried chicken with sriracha maple syrup or the more indulgent option of Nutella and banana.

Pancake picture: Lewis King

CULTIVATING A COUNTRYSIDE DESTINATION

With three dining options alongside rooms and a leisure club, Park Farm Hotel is an ideal spot for retreating into rural bliss just a few miles from Norwich.

Park Farm Hotel began life as a working farm complete with livestock, chickens, and a Georgian farmhouse which then became the focal point of a thriving business when owners Peter and Helen turned a few rooms into a B&B. Their son David now runs the business and that family feel is integral to the welcoming atmosphere at Park Farm Hotel. As it has grown, more accommodation and dining spaces have been added to create a countryside retreat – complete with its own spa and hair salon – that welcomes all visitors, whether for a meal, day trip or longer stay.

Seasons Restaurant, situated within the hotel and boasting an AA Rosette, offers high end dining that uses local ingredients wherever possible. Dishes such as venison carpaccio, duo of Cromer crab, duck breast and cod loin feature on a refined menu that shows off the best of Norfolk's produce. Breakfast features free-range eggs from a farm just down the road, and Park Farm Hotel's own garden allows the chefs to pick fresh herbs and seasonal vegetables just meters from the kitchen. Over in the bar, the food is a more relaxed affair to create a nice contrast for guests, featuring steaks, burgers, risotto, fish and chips, and other favourites.

For daytime dining, there's no shortage of hearty lunch options and Park Farm Hotel is particularly proud of its afternoon tea, served in the Drawing Room which was renovated and decorated just for that purpose, giving the space a real sense of occasion. Pastry chef Navita whips up fresh scones, cakes, and desserts every day to be enjoyed with delicate finger sandwiches and loose leaf teas. For those after something stronger, the bar features a seasonal cocktail menu and a different guest ale every week – all local of course – and the carefully curated wine list includes East Anglian bottles which have gone down a treat.

Everyone is welcome throughout the hotel and the wide range of visitors includes locals from nearby Hethersett and Wymondham, leisure club members enjoying the spa, pool and gym, walkers enjoying the beautiful circular route through the hotel's surrounding countryside, and even four-legged friends in the self-catering cottage on site. From individually designed Scandi-style lodges to luxurious suites, not to mention the sheltered courtyard for al fresco dining in warmer weather, there's something to suit everyone. The close-knit team enjoy their environment just as much as its visitors, making Park Farm Hotel truly welcoming and a world away from the every day.

PAN FRIED GRESSINGHAM DUCK BREAST

Preparation time: 30 minutes | Cooking time: 1 hour 30 minutes | Serves 2

We are surrounded by an abundance of amazing local produce at Park Farm Hotel and one of our favourites is Gressingham Duck. Paired with a rich jus and roasted vegetables makes for a simple but delicious dish. We love to incorporate vegetables from our kitchen garden, so this recipe features a colourful beetroot purée too.

1 large beetroot (around 200g)
2 carrots
2 cloves of garlic
4 tenderstem broccoli
1 shallot
100ml madeira
200g chicken stock
2 Gressingham duck breasts
Knob of butter
Olive oil
Honey

For the beetroot purée
Preheat the oven to 200°c. Lightly oil the beetroot, wrap in foil and place on a baking tray. Roast for 50-60 minutes until tender, then leave to cool before peeling. Place the roasted beetroot in a blender with a tablespoon of olive oil and blend until smooth. Pass through a fine sieve if needed, then season with salt and pepper to taste.

For the roast vegetables
Cut the carrots in half lengthways and finely chop the garlic. Place in a roasting tin and toss the carrots in a lug of olive oil and the garlic with salt, pepper, and a drizzle of honey. Roast for 20 minutes until tender. In a separate roasting tin, toss the tenderstem broccoli in a lug of olive oil with salt and pepper to taste. When the carrots have been in the oven for 10 minutes, add the broccoli.

For the madeira jus
Finely chop the shallot and melt a knob of butter in a medium hot pan. Sweat the shallot for about 2 minutes until soft, then add the madeira and bring to the boil. Bring back down to a simmer and keep on the heat until it has reduced by half, about 3-5 minutes. Add the chicken stock and continue to simmer until the sauce has reduced by two thirds and is thick enough to coat the back of a metal spoon. Keep it warm while you finish the dish.

For the duck breast
Heat some olive oil in a pan while you score the skin on each duck breast with a sharp knife, and season them with salt and pepper.
Place the duck in the hot pan, skin side down, and fry for about 5 minutes until browned and crispy. Now turn it over and cook on the other side for a further 4 minutes. Remove from the pan and rest the duck for 10 minutes before serving.

To serve
Place a tablespoon of the beetroot purée on the plate and swipe it across with the back of the spoon. Cut the duck breasts in half lengthways and place on the purée. Place the roast carrots and broccoli on the plate and spoon over the jus to finish.

ALL HANDS ON DECK

Part of a small North Norfolk restaurant group called Gangway Restaurants, Quarter Deck Bottle Shop and Kitchen serves a wonderful array of local ingredients throughout the day, specialising in British tapas and fresh fish.

Located in the heart of Sheringham, the Quarter Deck Bottle Shop and Kitchen is part of a privately owned and operated group of five businesses scattered along the North Norfolk Coast. It is owned by Will Chandler and co-owned by head chef Ben Pert alongside sous-chef Logan Coatesworth, Ben's nephew.

Will, Ben, and Logan had long dreamed of opening a food-led business, and when the building next door to the Sheringham Gangway became available one lucky day in December of 2022, they jumped at the chance. In such a scenic location, The Quarter Deck's impressive blue building boasts views over the North Norfolk railway, and has its own south-facing, sunny courtyard and even a holiday apartment upstairs.

The Quarter Deck offers a variety of diverse and tantalising menus. The day begins at The Quarter Deck with brunch and lunch, followed by small plates and a British Tapas sharing menu available from the early evening. The team pride themselves on the fresh local ingredients they use, including crabs from Sheringham, local samphire, and fresh fish brought in by locals, all of which head straight onto the ever-changing menus.

The chefs themselves contribute to this variety, having a large array of cooking experiences that range from fine dining to street food. With a team of chefs such as these, The Quarter Deck's menu has influences from all over the world, with lots of inspiration to keep it fresh and unique.

While unique, The Quarter Deck works closely with the other businesses in its group. Just next door is The Gangway, a sister restaurant, from which The Quarter Deck gets its name. Taking inspiration from their nautical location, and from the gangway and quarterdeck which join together on a ship, the name of the restaurant acknowledges their partnership – as does their recognisable anchor logo.

WARM ARTICHOKE SALAD WITH DILL YOGHURT DRESSING

Preparation time: 10 minutes | Cooking time: 20 minutes | Serves 4

A beautiful summer salad packed with flavour and fresh ingredients,
this is easy to make but tastes divine!

500g fresh broad beans, podded

300g fresh peas, podded

Salt

2 tbsp Mother's Garden extra virgin olive oil

10 artichoke hearts, from a jar, drained and halved

3 cloves of garlic, crushed

2 small dried chillies, crumbled

Sprig of rosemary, chopped

Sprig of oregano leaves, chopped

Zest and juice of 1 lemon

For the yoghurt dressing

A small handful of chopped dill

Zest and juice of 1 lemon

300g Greek yoghurt

1 clove of garlic, crushed

Salt and pepper

Tip the podded beans and peas into a pan of boiling salted water. Cook for 2 minutes.

Drain the beans and peas, then refresh them in ice cold water. Once they have cooled, drain them again.

Heat the olive oil in a pan over a medium heat. Add the artichoke hearts and cook for 2-3 minutes until they start to char. Then add the crushed garlic, crumbled chilli, rosemary, and oregano.

Allow the garlic to brown a little, then stir in the broad beans and peas. Gently warm them through, then add the lemon zest and juice. Remove the mixture from the heat, and season to taste.

To make the yoghurt dressing, combine all the ingredients in a bowl and mix well.

Arrange the warm salad in a serving bowl and spoon the dill yoghurt on top.

NORWICH'S FINE DINING SHOWCASE

A Norfolk institution, Roger Hickman has been showcasing modern British fine dining at his Norwich restaurant for well over a decade.

Roger Hickman opened his eponymous restaurant in 2010, but his reputation in Norwich goes back much further than that. Opening his own establishment marked his return to the city after a spell spent in London working with several top chefs, including Tom Aikens, who himself is a Norwich lad.

Originally from Leeds, Roger initially only took a catering course because he was too young to become a fireman, which was his childhood ambition. Fortunately, he discovered a natural talent in the kitchen – as well as a passion for fine dining. Roger was head chef at the renowned Adlards in Norwich, housed in the very building which now has his own name over the door, and is still the only restaurant in the city ever to hold a Michelin star.

He describes his style as 'modern British, with a twist', and his menus always demonstrate an accent on seasonal produce, with between 70 and 80% sourced in Norfolk. Roger admits to being a perfectionist, with French Laundry supremo Thomas Keller the chef he most admires. In 2018, he acquired the top two floors of the building and opened a smart private dining room on the first floor, seating up to 14 guests around one table. This has its own open kitchen, so that diners can watch Roger at work if they so wish. The main dining room on the ground floor is stylish and refined, with contemporary art (chosen by Roger, for whom art is another passion) on the walls, and smart white table linens. The impeccable front of house service, along with the food of course, is a large part of the reason that around half of the restaurant's visitors are regular customers.

The restaurant can claim to have the best wine list in Norfolk, having won the AA 'Notable Wine List' award five times, one of a select group of 120 establishments in the UK to hold the accolade, and the only one in Norfolk. The list contains nearly 100 wines, all of which are personally selected by Roger. Additionally, the restaurant has held three AA Rosettes since 2012 (the first in the city to achieve the accolade), was voted number 52 in the Square Meal Best UK Restaurants survey and won The Good Food Guide's Best Restaurant in East Anglia.

ROAST COD WITH CHICKPEA AND CHORIZO STEW

Preparation time: 2 hours 30 minutes | Cooking time: 50 minutes | Serves 4

The various different elements in this recipe work together to make it greater than the sum of its parts.
The simple chickpea and chorizo stew complements the fish perfectly, and the parsley crust – which
melts over the cooked cod – provides a showstopping and delicious garnish.

480g cod fillet, skinned

200g dry chickpeas

1 chorizo sausage, diced into 5mm pieces

300ml chicken stock

235g butter

200ml double cream

3 large turnips, peeled and sliced

10 sprigs of thyme

1 large red onion, peeled and cut into 4 slices (1cm thick)

2 tomatoes, quartered

1 tsp dried oregano

½ tsp sweet smoked paprika

Splash of white balsamic vinegar

Handful of flat leaf parsley

100g Panko breadcrumbs

Roll the cod fillet in clingfilm and chill in the fridge for 2 hours then cut into 4 equal portions. Meanwhile, soak the chickpeas in water for at least 2 hours, then drain. Boil the chickpeas in fresh water for 30-40 minutes; they should still have a slight bite. When cooked, drain again.

Sweat the chorizo in a dry pan, then add 25ml chicken stock and 10g butter. Reduce by half, then add 100ml double cream and the cooked chickpeas. Heat gently, and keep warm.

To make the turnip purée, sweat the chopped turnips in 125g butter for five minutes. Add the thyme, and cover with chicken stock. Reduce by half, then add 100ml double cream. Blitz in a food processor, and then pass through a fine sieve to give you a smooth purée. Keep warm.

Sear the onion in a pan with a little oil, with another pan directly on top to keep the onion slices flat. Transfer to an oven at 180°c and cook for 8 minutes.

Put the tomatoes, oregano, paprika and balsamic vinegar in a small oven tray and mix with your hands until the tomatoes are covered. Dry these out in a low oven for about 30 minutes.

To make the parsley crust, blitz the parsley and Panko breadcrumbs in a food processor, then add 100g melted butter. Roll the mixture between two sheets of parchment paper so that it is 3mm thick. Chill in the fridge.

Now cook the fish. Pan fry the cod pieces in oil for 2-3 minutes each side, then put in the oven at 180°c for 2 minutes. Remove from the oven and put a round of parsley crust on each piece of cod. The heat from the fish will melt the crust.

To serve, spoon some turnip purée on the plate, and then some of the chickpea and chorizo stew. Now arrange the crusted cod, two pieces of confit tomato, and one slice of red onion on each plate. You can garnish this dish with whatever you like – I use pickled turnip slices, chorizo oil and red amaranth.

SEASONAL DINING IN A HISTORIC SETTING

Set within the iconic mill where Colman's Mustard began life, Stoke Mill Restaurant is a piece of Norfolk history which is now home to award-winning food in beautiful surroundings.

There has been a mill at Stoke Holy Cross for 700 years, and it was here that Jeremiah and James Colman began making their world-famous mustard over 200 years ago. The mill was bought by the Iaccarino family in 1969 and was run as a successful high-class restaurant for over 40 years. In September 2013, Ludovico Iaccarino took over the family business in partnership with chef Andrew Rudd. They decided to invest in the historic premises to reinvent the restaurant for modern diners; sympathetic to the character of the mill, they restored and revealed original features and complemented the stunning space with solid oak tables and soft pastel hues.

Local support for Stoke Mill Restaurant has always been strong, and never more so than during the pandemic, when they offered a takeaway service and coffee stop/bakery counter. It was also during this time that Ludo and Andy joined forces with Norfolk-born chef Liam Nichols and set up STORE, the tasting menu restaurant nestled in the old storeroom of the building and a perfect hideaway for their newly Michelin-starred tasting menu.

Meanwhile, The Mill continues to be a busy and bustling restaurant, offering a du jour and à la carte menu, with the focus on great food in a relaxed atmosphere. Chef patron Andy Rudd uses local produce whenever he can; he loves to work with organic farmers and local producers to bring the best of the region's bounty into the kitchen. The chefs change the menu often, taking inspiration from the seasonal ingredients on their doorstep amidst Norfolk's bountiful countryside.

TWICE BAKED SMOKED NORFOLK DAPPLE SOUFFLÉ

Preparation time: 1 hour | Cooking time: 20-25 minutes | Serves 12

This has been on our menu for many years now as a firm favourite with customers old and new! Such a delicate and smooth starter, it's enough to whet anyone's appetite, with simple ingredients and a nod to Stoke Mill Restaurant's links to Colman's Mustard.

135g softened butter
185g sifted flour
500ml milk
1 white onion
3 bay leaves
1 head of garlic
3 egg yolks, beaten
1 large tsp Colman's mustard
170g Smoked Norfolk Dapple Cheese
6 egg whites
100ml double cream
100g grated cheddar

Lightly butter 12 soufflé moulds with 50g of the softened butter, brushing upwards, then lightly sprinkle with around 100g of the flour and tap to remove any excess.

Infuse the milk by placing it in a pan with the onion, bay leaves, and garlic to warm through slowly. Melt the remaining 85g of butter in a pan, add the remaining sifted flour and cook slowly on a gentle heat for around 5 minutes.

Strain the infused milk, discarding the solids, then pour it slowly into the roux in three stages, mixing well between each addition. Use a whisk rather than a spoon to prevent any lumps. Allow the sauce to cook on a low heat, then remove from the heat and fold in the egg yolks, mustard and cheese.

Season the sauce with salt and pepper to taste, then transfer the mixture into a large bowl and cover with cling film. In a separate bowl, whisk the egg whites until stiff, then gently fold them into the béchamel mixture until incorporated smoothly.

Lightly spoon or pipe the soufflé mixture into the prepared moulds, leaving a good centimetre at the top for the soufflés to rise. Bake them in a bain-marie at 150°c for 12-15 minutes, then allow to cool. Remove the soufflés from the moulds and place on greaseproof squares, ready for the fridge. Place in the fridge and keep for up to 3 days.

For the second bake, find a suitable ovenproof dish and place the soufflés on top of cooked spinach or leeks. Cover with the double cream and sprinkle the grated cheddar on top, then bake for 10 minutes until golden. Serve immediately.

THE BEST THINGS COME IN SMALL PACKAGES

This tiny Michelin-starred restaurant in Stoke Holy Cross, just outside of Norwich city centre, offers the coolest, most relaxed, and most fun chef's table experience in Norfolk.

The small back room of Stoke Mill, a well-known eatery set within a 700 year old mill, was transformed into a restaurant within a restaurant to create STORE in 2020. Experienced chef Liam – returning from overseas and living back home in Norwich due to the pandemic – teamed up with Andy and Ludo at Stoke Mill to produce takeaway hampers during the first lockdown, and a conversation at the pub evolved into the idea of establishing a tasting menu restaurant where they had formerly offered a private dining room. Following a full renovation, it opened for just a couple of weeks before the second lockdown hit, then finally got going in May 2021 when hospitality was able to reopen across the country.

Liam, a chef of 15 years, had previously cooked in many exciting kitchens around the world, including Midsummer House in Cambridge, Sat Bains in Nottingham, Press Club in Melbourne, Momofuku Ko in New York, Kerridge's Bar and Grill in London, and Necker Island in the British Virgin Islands. He heads up the kitchen at STORE, putting fun food with a global influence on the plates, alongside Hazel, the only other chef. She made the brave plunge into the world of professional cookery by embarking on an apprenticeship with Liam, completed shortly before STORE won its first Michelin star in 2023.

The intimate restaurant is where mustard used to be stored before being made into Colman's infamous condiment, hence the name STORE. Fast-forward 200 years and that same room is now home to a modern kitchen, five smartly dressed tables and a funky house playlist. The food takes the form of a seasonal tasting menu with optional wine pairings, all prepared in front of the guests and served by Liam and Hazel themselves. Liam describes their style as "without a rulebook" but featuring lots of Asian influences drawn from his travels and past experiences. As such, tasty food with worldwide flavours is always the order of the day, embracing produce from across the globe alongside local favourites and Liam's pick of ingredients from nearby Asian supermarkets.

"I'm still learning every day and opening STORE was a huge learning curve," explains Liam. "One of the hardest things as a team of just two is developing new dishes; Hazel and I do this regularly so we can add things to the menu once another dish is ready to come off, or we get new seasonal ingredients coming through. I couldn't do what we do without Hazel, who is a superstar, and we are beyond proud to have achieved a Michelin star already – I still can't quite believe it!"

ROASTED SCALLOP WITH THAI GREEN CURRY SAUCE AND DAIKON SALAD

Preparation time: 10-15 minutes | Cooking time: 15-20 minutes | Serves 4

For a vegan version of this delicious dish, switch out the scallop for courgette.

4 scallops (or courgette pieces)
2 shallots, chopped
2 cloves of garlic, chopped
1 lemongrass stick, gently bashed
1 nugget of ginger, chopped
1 green chilli, chopped
2 tbsp sesame oil
2 tsp Thai green curry paste
1 tin of full-fat coconut milk
1 bunch of coriander, chopped
1 handful of spinach
1 small daikon
1 red chilli
2 tbsp rice vinegar
Vegetable oil
Handful of toasted chopped peanuts
Spoonful of toasted coconut

First, clean the scallops (or chop the courgette into scallop-shaped rounds) and set aside.

To make the Thai green curry sauce, place the shallot, garlic, lemongrass, ginger and green chilli in a pan with a splash of the sesame oil and sweat until soft.

Add the curry paste and cook for a further minute, then pour in the coconut milk and simmer for 4 minutes. Stir in the coriander and spinach, simmer until just wilted, then transfer to a blender and blend until smooth. Set aside ready for plating (or chill to save the sauce for later).

To make the salad, cut the daikon into matchstick-sized pieces. Finely chop the red chilli and then mix the daikon and chilli with the remaining sesame oil and rice vinegar.

Next, cook the scallops (or courgette rounds) in a pan with a little vegetable oil until golden.

To plate the dish, spoon some warmed Thai green curry sauce into the bottom of a bowl, sit the scallop (or courgette) in the centre and then place some daikon salad on top. Garnish with the peanuts and coconut. Serve and enjoy!

MUCH MORE THAN A DELI!

Thornham Deli is a one-stop destination on the North Norfolk coast where you can enjoy the best local cuisine, shop 'til you drop in the lifestyle store, and even spend the night in a sumptuous suite.

A thriving independent business with many strings to its bow, Thornham Deli is the place to eat, drink, shop and stay in North Norfolk. Their extensive menu offers a broad range of daytime favourites to cater for all tastes, including the ever-popular traditional Deli Breakfast, alongside healthy nourish bowls, light bites, pancakes and more. With seasonal changes every six months, Executive Head Chef Gemma Arnold also creates daily specials using the freshest local produce, such as locally-caught fish or top-quality meat and vegetables in the curry of the week. Having been a chef for 23 years, Gemma draws on her immense experience across a wide range of cateries to reinvent popular dishes with her own inimitable twist. Gemma has also created, and continues to expand, the Deli own brand – TD Kitchen – which is available to buy in the food store. The Deli counter is bursting with homemade savoury and sweet delicacies from their famous Scotch eggs to the delicious millionaire's shortbread.

Alongside Gemma, the team at Thornham Deli work hard to maintain their high standards across the board. Janie, Jeanne and Derek are the big bosses – Jeanne and Derek travel extensively, bringing back new ideas and inspiration, and Janie is the woman on the ground – while Front of House Manager Denise Le Gallez heads up their 40+ members of staff. Accounts and the all-important paperwork are handled by Donna Raven, who has been working with Janie for over 20 years and is referred to as 'her right arm'! Janie was offered the opportunity to buy the Deli back when she was a customer herself, popping in for a coffee before going to work – as they say, the rest is history...

The busy, fast-moving venture has been flourishing ever since, with a sister business – No33 Boutique Holiday Accommodation – opening around the same time. No33 provides luxurious suites and cottages along the Norfolk coast, including 4 suites above the Deli.

The Deli is also home to a lifestyle store, including an interior design service. The owners' flair for aesthetically pleasing décor is reflected throughout the Deli itself, where different styles of furniture – from lamps to comfy chairs, as well as local art – are curated, not just to enjoy while eating but to purchase too.

"We always strive to be the best and are constantly recreating ourselves in keeping with our original ethos," explains Janie. "We visit as many shows as possible, in search of the next new thing or a better approach, as we are all so passionate about what we do and want to deliver the best of everything to our band of supportive customers."

#
DELI CHICKEN CAESAR BURGER

Preparation time: 30-40 minutes | Cooking time: 15-20 minutes | Serves 4

Our customer favourite, the Deli Burger, has gained a sister! Thanks to an epiphany from our executive head chef, our Deli Chicken Caesar Burger offers a healthy alternative that still packs a punch. The Norfolk quail eggs are a great accompaniment to the anchovy dressing laced with angostura bitters and parmesan.

For the burgers

4 chicken breasts, skinned and boned
50g plain flour
Salt and pepper
2 whole eggs, beaten
100g panko breadcrumbs
8 rashers of streaky bacon
4 brioche buns
4 bamboo skewers

For the Caesar dressing

4 egg yolks
2 anchovy fillets
50g parmesan, grated
1 lemon, juiced
1 tbsp Worcestershire sauce
1 tsp Tabasco
½ tsp angostura bitters
150ml olive oil
150ml vegetable oil

For the Caesar salad

8 quail eggs
2 baby gem lettuces
25g parmesan
8 anchovy fillets

For the burgers

Butterfly each chicken breast, season the plain flour with salt and pepper, then coat each piece of chicken in the flour. Now dip them into the beaten egg, followed by the panko breadcrumbs. Gently heat your frying pan with a dash of oil and fry the breadcrumbed chicken until lightly golden on both sides. Transfer to a preheated oven at 180°c for 10-15 minutes.

For the Caesar dressing

Prepare this while the burgers are cooking (it could also be made in advance). Place the egg yolks, anchovies and grated parmesan into a food processor. Start to blend, add the lemon juice, Worcestershire sauce, Tabasco, and bitters, then gradually pour in the oils with the blender running to form a mayonnaise-like consistency. Season the dressing to taste, then set aside.

For the Caesar salad

Boil the quail eggs for 2 minutes, then refresh under cold water and peel. Separate, wash and dry the baby gem leaves, then shred and place in a mixing bowl. Add your Caesar dressing and toss to combine. Use a peeler to shave the parmesan and set everything aside separately.

To plate and serve

Grill or fry the streaky bacon rashers until crisp. Slice the brioche buns in half and lightly toast them under a grill or in a dry pan (they won't take long due to the high content of butter in the dough).

Place the toasted bun base on the plate, spoon on the dressed lettuce, then place the chicken burger on top followed by 2 rashers of streaky bacon, 2 anchovy fillets, and some parmesan shavings. Add a second spoonful of dressed lettuce, place the bun lid on top, then carefully skewer 2 quail eggs and use this to secure the burger from the top down. Repeat to make the others and serve with fries.

RETREAT AND RELAX

Tucked away in the North Norfolk coastal village of Cley-next-the-Sea,
The Three Swallows is an idyllic place to enjoy a quintessentially British
pub menu along with your favourite tipple.

The Three Swallows has existed as a pub since at least 1789, made it through centuries of challenges from flooding to the pandemic, and is now in the capable hands of experienced manager Matt Drew. Formerly overseeing three other pubs in the area, Matt decided to bite the bullet in January 2023 when he took over from the previous landlord. The Three Swallows has since been brought up to date with a complete refurbishment – to the approval of its customers, who love the contemporary feel alongside all the character that has been retained – and a growing reputation for great food.

You might describe the menu as premium gastropub fare with an adventurous side; the options range from bar snacks and mezze plates to homemade pies and stone-baked pizza. Classic dishes comfortably rub shoulders with modern bistro and international influences, creating a relaxed eatery that's bound to have something for everyone. Nibble on katsu bonbons or Padron peppers with drinks, sit down to a hearty ploughman's lunch after a seaside walk or bike ride, or treat yourself to the whole hog with starters, mains, puds and even a British cheeseboard for a memorable evening.

If the weather allows, all this can be enjoyed on the pub's patio and lawn, complete with an outdoor pizza oven and bar, for the perfect al fresco experience. With space for up to 300 people outside and more in the cosy interior, there's no shortage of spots to enjoy Norfolk's best cask ales – Matt is always keen to source locally produced food and drink where he can, from the county's favourite beers to seasonal farm shop vegetables and seafood from Cley Smokehouse. He also hopes to secure a wedding licence for the future, building on the many attributes The Three Swallows can already boast as an events venue, not least the garden's view of spectacular sunsets over Cley.

Thanks to their ambition and dedication, Matt and his team – which includes his brother, Gareth – have started to see locals coming back to the pub who haven't been for years, and they are grateful for their many regular visitors alongside the walkers, birdwatchers, families, and dog owners who are all welcomed in this "hidden gem" off the main coast road. "We're keen to put our name on the map and grow the business," says Matt, "so I'm looking forward to meeting all the new challenges that come our way to make The Three Swallows everything it can be."

PEA AND MINT RISOTTO

Preparation time: 10 minutes | Cooking time: 40-50 minutes | Serves 2

This recipe has always been a huge success with customers and is very adaptable depending on the season. It's great throughout the summer months but is warming enough to be enjoyed on a cold day too, as well as being an ideal base for many other dishes such as fish.

25g butter

1 shallot, finely chopped

2 cloves of garlic, finely chopped

175g risotto rice

100ml white wine

150g frozen peas

850ml vegetable stock

Salt and pepper, to taste

13g parmesan, grated (or a vegan/vegetarian alternative)

Handful of fresh mint, finely chopped

Handful of pea shoots

Drizzle of olive oil

In a large pan, melt the butter over a low heat. Add the finely chopped shallot and garlic, gently sweat for about 10 minutes until soft, then stir in the risotto rice.

Increase the heat to medium and cook the rice for 1 minute. Pour in the wine and stir until the rice has absorbed the liquid. Add the peas and give the mixture a gentle stir.

Add a ladleful of the vegetable stock and continue cooking the risotto, stirring continuously and adding another ladleful of stock once the previous one has been absorbed, until the rice is tender and has a good creamy consistency. This process will take about 20-30 minutes.

Taste the risotto, then season with salt and pepper as needed. Gently stir in the parmesan, then add the chopped mint and fold it through the risotto.

Finally, spoon the risotto into shallow bowls and top with the pea shoots and a drizzle of good olive oil.

TIPPLES, VEGETABLES AND MORE

Norfolk's place-to-be for delicious, internationally inspired vegan food that's brought to you fresh from the kitchen. Not just a restaurant, their cocktail bar offers impressive and unique drinks if you get thirsty.

The Tipsy Vegan is a restaurant and cocktail bar concept that opened in Norwich in 2017. It was launched by founders Michelle McCabe and Cheryl Mullenger, who were already operating a hugely popular Americana lunch business, Bia Vegan Diner, from Norwich Market.

The Tipsy Vegan proudly pushes the boundaries of vegan eating and drinking with internationally inspired dishes. A commitment to consistently providing excellent quality food and drink forms the foundation of this restaurant, with an emphasis on quality core ingredients. They stand out from the crowd by ensuring that their dishes and drinks are made in-house as much as possible. That way, customers get to experience flavour combinations exclusive to the Tipsy Vegan menu. It's hard work, but the Tipsy Vegan team is dedicated to producing a truly unique experience for customers that cannot be easily replicated.

Founders Michelle and Cheryl have vastly different backgrounds but together hold a plethora of skills which complement one another, enabling the business to stay current and creative. Michelle has been in the hospitality sector for over 20 years, with culinary experience at all levels, having worked in venues across the US and in London. She has been vegan for over 7 years and is the driving force behind the expansion plans for the company.

Cheryl Mullenger was a secondary school teacher for 11 years prior to launching the company and has an avid interest in nutrition and health. She has created and developed from scratch all of the famous recipes that are exclusive to the business and extremely popular.

The inspiration for Tipsy's food and drink is twofold. First, they are inspired by a love of travel and experiencing new cultures, flavour combinations and getting excited about trying to recreate them. They are also inspired by a desire to 'veganise' dishes or meals that are regularly enjoyed with family and friends, creating plant-based replicas that may even surpass the original. For the Tipsy Vegan, this is always the key objective.

SMOKEY ANCHO QUESADILLA MIX

Preparation time: 10 minutes | Cooking time: 25 minutes | Serves 2

This mix is highly versatile. It is great for quesadillas but can also be used in burritos,
tacos, with rice or as a filling for empanadas. Enjoy!

125g onion

75g red pepper

75g yellow pepper

2 stalks of celery

1g garlic

350g sweet potatoes

Splash of olive oil

1 tbsp ancho chilli powder

1 tbsp smoked paprika

1 tbsp cumin

100g tomato purée

400ml stock

200g black beans

50g coriander

2 tsp salt

Tortilla wraps

Vegan mozzarella

Dice the onion, peppers, celery, garlic, and sweet potatoes into small pieces/cubes. The sweet potatoes don't need to be peeled unless desired - simply wash and remove any unwanted parts.

Add the onion, peppers, celery, and garlic to a medium sized saucepan and sauté on a medium heat with a little olive oil until the veg has softened.

Add in the sweet potato cubes and continue to allow the veg to soften.

While the veg is cooking, measure out all the spices and tomato purée in a separate bowl. Make up the required amount of stock, drain the black beans, and finely chop the coriander including the stalks so they are all ready when needed.

Add the tomato purée and spices to the pan and cook until the spices become fragrant. You may want to reduce the heat so the spices don't burn. Stir thoroughly so all of the veg is coated.

After a few minutes, add in the black beans and stir again, ensuring they are covered in spices.

Now add the stock, coriander and salt and bring to a simmer. Continue to simmer, stirring often to avoid the mixture sticking to the bottom, until the sweet potato is cooked. Remove from the heat. Add seasoning if required.

To build your quesadilla, sprinkle the desired amount of vegan mozzarella on one half of a tortilla wrap. Then add 2-3 tablespoons of Smokey Ancho Mix along the centre of the wrap and on top of the cheese, away from the wrap's edges. Add another layer of mozzarella on top and fold your wrap in half. The mixture should be in the middle of the wrap so use your hand to push it to the top, forcing the mix to fill the whole area while keeping it all inside the wrap.

Place the quesadilla onto a hot pan/griddle/hot plate and allow it to heat through, melting the cheese and charring the exterior of the tortilla. Remove it from the heat and let it cool slightly before serving.

LIFTING THE LID ON RELAXED FINE DINING

An award-winning relaxed fine dining restaurant in the village of Stoke Holy Cross close to Norwich, this Michelin Recommended destination brings together dishes using all that is great and good from Norfolk.

South Norfolk Chef Daniel Smith purchased The Wildebeest in 2015, bringing it under G&D Ventures, Norfolk's Independent Hospitality Group, alongside The Ingham Swan. The Wildebeest has always been much loved and over the years it has transitioned from an African themed restaurant, under previous owners, through to its current calm and neutral palette. The Wildebeest is ideally situated close to central Norwich and its design evokes a laid-back yet sophisticated atmosphere. The dining space is relaxed to include banquette seating, giving the restaurant a sense of space throughout its open-plan dining area, with a secluded, al fresco dining area and a classy fine dining restaurant inside.

Under Head Chef Fabio Miani, The Wildebeest has, for many years, enjoyed an enviable reputation for food and drink and is one of Norfolk's best-loved restaurants, consistently delivering on its relaxed fine dining promise. Awarded Norfolk Chef of the Year in 2019, with a reputation as one of Norfolk's most creative young chefs, Italian-born Fabio says his passion for cooking began while watching his father cooking at home for the family. He joined The Wildebeest in 2018, after working at several top award-winning restaurants in Italy and England, and leads the talented kitchen team; "I am proud to be at the helm of an always energetic and endlessly talented kitchen."

Fabio carefully creates every menu to take full advantage of the wide range of local produce that is available on the doorstep, from land to sea; bringing together dishes that embrace every season with daily changing menus across lunch and dinner, à la carte, Sunday lunch and tasting menus. Fabio buys the very best locally and seasonally – working with trusted suppliers who offer quality ingredients, such as local small-scale growers Tilia Veg, a vegetable farm growing chemical-free produce, nearby in Hempnall. The Wildebeest also has its own small growing garden to give the kitchen team the opportunity to learn more about the growing process. The kitchen team also love to forage for ingredients with wild garlic being one of their favourites.

Menus include many Wildebeest favourites as well as brand new dishes created in the kitchen. The Wildebeest has an exceptionally strong suit when it comes to pastry with many customers raving about its desserts. Alongside the tasting menus, described as a delight for all the senses, a wine pairing service is available to take diners on a perfectly paired wine journey.

DUCK, CREAMED POTATOES AND CRISPY MUSHROOMS

Preparation time: 2 hours | Cooking time: 20 minutes | Serves 4

Head Chef Fabio shares a seasonal recipe that really packs a flavour punch. "Everything I serve from the kitchen takes its cue from the current season. The colder months bring us new food sources to forage and work with in the kitchen. Fresh ingredients and cold season favourites like beetroot and mushrooms are a real favourite of mine." You can simplify this recipe as needed.

For the mashed potato

10 potatoes
250g whole milk
250g double cream
200g salted butter

For the duck

4 beetroots
2 bunches of enoki mushrooms
50g butter
Vegetable oil for frying
4 duck breasts
20g thyme
2 cloves of garlic
250g curly kale, stems removed
Salt and pepper to taste

Start by making the mashed potato. Oven-bake the potatoes at 180°c for about an hour until soft all the way through. Meanwhile, in a separate pan go ahead and boil the beetroot adding enough water to completely cover them. Bring to the boil and continuously check that they are always fully submerged in water.

While the beetroot is being prepared, heat up the whole milk in a pan, adding in the cream and salted butter, on a low heat and season with salt, pepper, thyme and garlic to infuse the flavours. Once up to the boil, keep warm until needed and set aside.

Remove the potatoes from the oven and while they are still hot, cut in half and scoop the cooked potato out, then pass through a fine sieve to achieve a nice and smooth consistency. Then, in a separate pan, take the potatoes, the infused buttery milk (strain it first) and give it a good mix all together. Once happy with flavour and consistency, set the mash aside to be used later.

Back to the beetroot. Once cooked, drain and carefully peel. Cut into small pieces and blitz in a blender with 50g of butter, with salt and pepper to taste, until silky smooth. Pass through a fine sieve if required for extra smoothness and set aside for later.

To prepare the enoki mushrooms (or a mushroom of your choice) trim the end of the bunch, which will allow these small, stemmed mushrooms to fall and separate from each other. In a pan, preheat the vegetable oil to 170°c and deep fry the mushrooms until golden. Once fried, season with salt and set aside.

With all the garnish prepared, it's now time to prep and cook the duck. Before cooking duck breasts, it is always recommended to score the skin with a knife; this will help the fat to render from the skin, making it crispier, and it also prevents the meat from curling up during cooking. Season the duck breasts with salt and pepper and add them into a cold non-stick pan with the skin side down. Add a very small touch of vegetable oil and starting with a low-medium heat, render all the fat from the skin.

Once golden and crispy turn the duck in the pan, adding a generous knob of butter along with the thyme and garlic, and baste the breast for a couple of minutes before removing from the pan and placing into a hot oven for 3-4 minutes at 180°c. Once cooked, let the duck rest for at least 5 minutes before slicing.

While the duck breast is resting, blanch the curly kale in salted boiling water and reheat the potato ready to serve.

To serve the dish, spread some beetroot purée on the bottom of a plate, place the kale in the middle and then sit the sliced duck breast on top of it. Garnish with more kale. I like to pop some pickled turnips on the plate too. You can serve the potato on the side or on the plate topping it with your crispy mushroom.

THE WOOLF OF NELSON STREET

In 2015, Francis Woolf and Felix Rehberg created Woolf & Social. They decided that Norwich's food scene had space for an affordable restaurant that could showcase the finest ingredients Norfolk has to offer in new and innovative ways.

The concept of Woolf & Social is to bring fine dining quality and cooking techniques to a new audience by making food the centre of the experience. The restaurant is minimally decorated: the crockery and cutlery doesn't always match, and the chairs and tables are salvaged from an old school, but no expense is spared on the quality of ingredients. This is what makes them special – high-end but affordable food.

Francis used to frequent a social club during his youth, where drinks and food were inexpensive, "The atmosphere was easy-going, relaxed, social. We would all know one another, and it became a kind of community space that was centred around food and drinks - that's what I wanted for the restaurant, hence the word 'social' in the name."

You can find Woolf & Social tucked behind Dereham Road, which is a very residential area. It's not the usual spot for a restaurant, but that's part of its allure. It's a neighbourhood restaurant in the truest sense, and why they won The Good Food Guide's Best Local Restaurant Award for this region.

As the restaurant is small, the experience is intimate and warm. The team of staff are extremely knowledgeable about the food, including Benedict Hemmens who has curated a thoughtful list of wines and cocktails.

The menu changes frequently depending on seasonality and availability of local ingredients. There is a strong Asian influence here, drawing on Francis' background in Japanese and Southeast Asian Cuisine. There are a few menu staples though, including Smacked Cucumbers (a cucumber salad from the Sichuan province), Fried Chicken (voted best in the country on Channel 4's Sunday Brunch), and Chocolate Cake (gluten-free and melt-in-the-mouth).

Over lockdown, Woolf & Social capitalised on its outside space, creating a terrace filled with wisteria and grapevines. This put them in The Times' Top 40 places to eat outside in the UK. Francis' dedication to making food inclusive also saw them land a spot in The Times' Top 40 vegetarian destinations. They have also had fantastic reviews in The Guardian, The Telegraph, Time Out, Waitrose Magazine, and many others. It's clear that their award from The Good Food Guide means the most to them though, as it stands proudly right by the entrance!

PORK, APPLE AND MISO

Preparation time: 15 minutes, plus 30 minutes before serving | Cooking time: 4 hours, plus cooling overnight | Serves 5

This gluten-free recipe is simple, impressive and delicious. It was inspired by a dish from Sushi Leblon in Rio! East Anglia produces some of the best pork in the world, and I encourage everyone to procure their meat from a local butcher. Support small independents or lose them!

For the meat

4 tbsp Chinese five spice

2 tbsp fennel seeds

2 tbsp sea salt

2 tbsp sugar, any kind

1.5 kg pork belly, ribs and skin removed (ask your butcher to do this)

1 large onion

4 star anises

50ml rice vinegar

50ml gluten-free soy sauce

100ml white wine or mirin

500ml neutral oil (sunflower, maize or rapeseed)

100ml blended sesame oil (optional)

For the sauce

200g white miso (gf)

100ml rice vinegar

2 tbsp sugar

Splash of cold water

For the salad

5 firm British apples (Norfolk and Suffolk grow incredible apples, ask your grocer for a firm variety)

Splash of rice or cider vinegar

2 tbsp toasted white sesame seeds

Splash of sesame oil

Preheat your oven to 130°c, then mix the five spice, fennel seeds, salt and sugar.

Score the fatty side of the belly (the paler side) with a knife, then rub the seasoning into every crevice and cranny, coating it evenly. Afterwards, roughly chop the onion.

Take a roasting tray, wider and deeper than your pork belly, and spread the onion and the star anises over the base of the roasting tray. This will stop the meat from sticking.

Place the pork over the onion, fatty side up.

Pour the wet ingredients down the side of the meat (not over it). Pour the vinegar first, then the soy and wine, then the oil. The belly should be just proud of the oil.

Place a piece of baking parchment over the meat to prevent the tinfoil sticking, then take some tinfoil and tightly cover the roasting tray. Put in the oven for 4 hours.

After 4 hours, remove the pork. Being careful not to spill the hot oil, peel back a corner of the tinfoil and push a sharp knife into the meat. You should feel little to no resistance. Remove the knife and leave the pork to cool.

Once your pork belly is at room temperature, remove it from the oil and place it on a baking tray that will fit in your fridge. Keep the oil aside for later. Tightly wrap in clingfilm (the aim here is to compress the pork so it firms up again in the fridge). Leave the pork in the fridge overnight.

30 minutes before serving, combine the miso, vinegar, sugar and a splash of water in a bowl and whisk until the sugar has completely dissolved.

In a separate bowl, grate or finely slice your apples into matchsticks. Immediately mix with a splash of vinegar to prevent them from browning. Toss in the sesame seeds and sesame oil, then mix gently.

Take a large frying pan, preferably non-stick, and add 3 tablespoons of the oil that your pork was cooked in. Turn to a low heat.

Take the cooled pork and slice it into 2-3cm deep strips across the grain of the pork. These can be trimmed to fit your pan. Add your strips of pork to the pan 4 or 5 at a time.

Turn up the heat and crisp the pork, turning occasionally with tongs until the meat is brown on both sides. Repeat as necessary.

To serve, arrange your apple salad down the centre of the plate. Place blobs or flicks of the miso sauce around the plate - get creative with this! Now place the pork belly and serve.

DIRECTORY

THE CABIN
19 Pit Street, Southrepps, Norfolk, NR11 8UX
07525648940
www.thecabinnorfolk.com
Instagram @thecabinnorfolk
Asian inspired street food including tacos and curries from a converted 80s caravan.

CHET VALLEY VINEYARD
Loddon Road, Bergh Apton, Norwich, NR15 1BT
01508 333002
www.chetvineyard.co.uk
Instagram @chetvineyard
Family-run vineyard and winery in South Norfolk, producing award-winning wines and offering unforgettable experiences.

CHRISTOPHE'S CRÊPES
12A Pottergate, Norwich NR2 1DS
07581 420352
Facebook christophescrepes
Independent crêperie selling sweet and savoury pancakes to eat in or takeaway.

ELVEDEN FARMS LTD
Estate Office, London Office, Elveden, IP24 3TQ
01842 898068
www.elvedenestate.com
Find us on social media with #elvedenestate
Elveden Courtyard Farm Shop, Gift Shop and Restaurants, including the Dog & Scone, a dog-friendly café, situated on a farming estate which is home to the Guinness family.

FARMYARD
23 St Benedicts Street, Norwich, NR24PF
01603 733188
www.farmyard.restaurant
Find us on social media @farmyardrestaurant
Michelin listed restaurant that prides itself on fine produce and cares as much about their 'free-range chefs' as the high quality and sustainable produce. Spin off business Farmyard Frozen Ltd is the thinking person's frozen food product .

FIGBAR
23 St John Maddermarket, Norwich, NR2 1DN
www.figbarnorwich.com
hello@figbarnorwich.com
Instagram @figbarnorwich
Award-winning modern meeting place, where pre-theatre pick-me-ups shine and first dates don't have to end.

THE INGHAM SWAN RESTAURANT WITH ROOMS
Sea Palling Road, Ingham, Norfolk, NR12 9AB
01692 581099
www.theinghamswan.co.uk
Instagram @theinghamswan
14th-century inn with a fine dining restaurant, rustic-chic rooms and free gourmet breakfast.

THE KIMCHI
4a Brigg Street, Norwich, NR2 1QN
01603629215
www.thekimchi.co.uk
Facebook and Instagram @thekimchinorwich
A wide range of dishes to choose from, including Korean Fried Chicken, sizzling BBQ dishes and healthy Bibimbap bowls.

THE KINGS ARMS FLEGGBURGH
Main Road, Fleggburgh, Norfolk, NR29 3AG
01493 368333
www.kingsarmsfleggburgh.com
Instagram @thekingsarms_fleggburgh
Stunning destination restaurant with rooms open for breakfast, lunch and dinner with delicious food made in-house daily.

KINGS HEAD BAWBURGH
Harts Lane, Bawburgh, NR9 3LS
01603 744977
www.kingsheadbawburgh.co.uk
Instagram @kingsheadbawburgh
Owners for forty years, Anton Wimmer and his family pride themselves on their excellent reputation.

LOVE NORWICH FOOD & DRINK WALKING TOURS
Lodge Farm Holiday Barns, New Road, Bawburgh, Norwich, NR93LZ
01603 742247
www.lovenorwichfood.co.uk
Instagram @love_norwich_food
Having run a cookery school and been a food writer for many years, Zena established the tours to embrace Norfolk produce and showcase local independent restaurants and bars.

MINDFUL MIXOLOGY
Unit 2 Park Farm, Salle, NR10 4SG
07944166433
www.mindfulmixology.co.uk
Find us on social media @mindfulmixology_uk
Mindful Mixology make bottled 'ready to drink' cocktails with a difference. Made with less sugar, using small brands, vegan-friendly and winner of a Great Taste 3-star award.

MONTYS MUSTARDS AND CHUTNEYS
The Old Dairy, Manor Farm, Stanfield, Norfolk, NR20 4HY
01362668844
www.essencefoods.co.uk
Instagram @montys_mustards
Montys was created in 2017 to produce the highest quality mustards and chutneys possible from the Savage family team in the heart of Norfolk. Handmade artisanal products looking to reignite the country's love of mustard.

THE MULBERRY
11 Raymond Street, Thetford, Norfolk, IP24 2EA
01842 824122
www.mulberrythetford.co.uk
Facebook Mulberry Thetford
A friendly, tucked away, neighbourhood treat, The Mulberry is a discreet and welcoming business that focuses on delivering the best food from the finest locally-sourced ingredients.

NAMASTE VILLAGE

131-139 Queens Rd, Norwich, NR1 3PN
01603 466466
namasteindiannorwich.com
Vegetarian Indian dishes presented in classic, colourful surrounds with a bustling atmosphere.

THE OLD STORE SNETTISHAM

5 Pedlars Mews, Snettisham, PE31 7XQ
www.theoldstorenorfolk.co.uk
Facebook and Instagram @theoldstorenorfolk
A micro-bakery and coffee shop, serving delicious foods both in and on bread.

PARK FARM HOTEL

Norwich Road, Hethersett, NR9 3DL
01603 810264
www.parkfarm-hotel.co.uk
Find us on social media @parkfarmhotel
Park Farm Hotel and Leisure is a blissful rural retreat, hotel and spa set in 200 acres of idyllic countryside.

THE QUARTER DECK

Station House, 8 Station Approach, Sheringham, NR26 8RA
01263 826232
www.thequarterdeck.uk
Instagram @thequarterdecksheringham
A Bottle Shop and Kitchen in the heart of Sheringham, part of a privately owned group of five businesses along the north Norfolk coast.

ROGER HICKMAN'S RESTAURANT

79 Upper St Giles Street, Norwich, NR2 1AB
01603 633522
www.rogerhickmansrestaurant.com
Instagram @rogerhickmans
A Norfolk institution, Roger Hickman's has been showcasing modern British fine dining in a sophisticated atmosphere for over a decade.

SALT

21 St John Maddermarket, Norwich, NR2 1DN
www.saltnorwich.com
Find us on social media @saltnorwich
SALT is a made-from-scratch kitchen by chef-owner Jaime Garbutt, offering a variety of delectable sandwiches, salads, and plates that change with the seasons.

STOKE MILL RESTAURANT

Stoke Mill, Mill Road, Stoke Holy Cross, Norwich, Norfolk, NR14 8PA
01508 493337
www.stokemills.co.uk
Find us on social media @stokemill
Fine dining restaurant set in an old watermill, with an adjacent Michelin-starred tasting room.

STORE AT STOKE MILL

Stoke Mill, Mill Road, Stoke Holy Cross, Norwich, Norfolk, NR14 8PA
01508 493337
www.stokemillstore.co.uk
Find us on social media @stokemill_store
Michelin-starred chef's tasting room: a visual journey from the kitchen to the table born out of the pandemic.

THORNHAM DELI LTD

Thornham Deli, High Street, Thornham, Norfolk, PE36 6LX
01485 512194
www.thornhamdeli.co.uk
Facebook and Instagram Thornham Deli
A one-stop shop, restaurant, deli, clothing boutique, and stylish accommodation on the north Norfolk coast.

THE THREE SWALLOWS

Newgate Green, Cley-next-the-Sea, Holt, Norfolk, NR25 7TT
01263 740816
www.thethreeswallows.co.uk
A charming village pub nestled in the small market town of Cley, this coastal hidden gem offers a quintessential British menu coupled with classic beverages in a stylish traditional country setting.

THE TIPSY VEGAN

68-70 St Benedict's Street, Norwich, NR2 4AR
01603 666788
www.thetipsyvegan.co.uk
Instagram @thetipsyvegangroup
We push the boundaries of vegan dining, with internationally inspired dishes. Carefully sourced ingredients and fairtrade drinks come together to create delicious meals. You don't have to be tipsy or vegan to enjoy our food.

THE WILDEBEEST

82-86 Norwich Road, Stoke Holy Cross, Norwich, NR14 8QJ
01508 492497
www.thewildebeest.co.uk
Instagram @thewildebeestnorfolk
An award-winning, relaxed, fine dining restaurant in Stoke Holy Cross close to Norwich that brings together dishes using all that is great and good from Norfolk.

WOOLF & SOCIAL

21-23 Nelson Street, Norwich, NR2 4DW
01603 443658
www.woolfandsocial.co.uk
Instagram/Facebook/Twitter @woolfandsocial
A small neighbourhood restaurant serving sharing dishes, fine wines and cocktails. Francis Woolf's food is inspired by cuisines from around the world but focussed on local, seasonal ingredients.